The World is in Our Words

To Mike and Sue Atkins
Ahmed Gurnah, Abdul and Muna Shaif
the late Bill Walton CEO,
Derek Rose, Mick Poore
and Pedro Fuentes,
who gave me the hope
and strength to write
this book in grim and isolated times

The World is in Our Words
A Life in Poetry

Chris Searle

Five Leaves Publications
www.fiveleaves.co.uk

The World is in Our Words
A Life in Poetry
by Chris Searle

Published in 2022
by Five Leaves,

14a Long Row,
Nottingham NG1 2DH

www.fiveleaves.co.uk
www.fiveleavesbookshop.co.uk

ISBN 9781910170915

Typeset by 4 Sheets Design and Print

Printed in Great Britain

Contents

Introduction

The World is in Our Words is the second part of Chris Searle's story of his life, following *Isaac and I*. It begins in 1979, after he returned from teaching in Mozambique when the country was casting off Portuguese colonial rule. Back in Britain, from the 1980s, he resumed a long-term commitment to fostering a conscious creativity through education. Helped by the Greater London Council in 1984 he edited a collection of poems by London school children, *Our City*. Neil Kinnock launched it in the House of Commons and the children read out their poems. The *Daily Mail* was not happy, but a young Jeremy Corbyn staunchly defended them.

Turmoil and enthusiasm continued to surround Chris Searle's approach to education. In 1990, when he was appointed as head of Earl Marshal Comprehensive in a poor area of Sheffield, the Department of Education and Science, under the Tories, tried to get Sheffield to rescind the appointment. The city's Chief Education Officer resisted and Chris Searle went north, where he was affectionately called 'Duck' on the buses and his students came from families who had migrated from Kashmir, Mirpur in Pakistan, the Caribbean, the Yemen and Northern Somalia. Earl Marshal was truly a 'School of the World'.

Fervently opposed to racism, he quickly noted that disproportionate numbers of black children were being excluded from schools and took a firm stand as head against permanent expulsions. Instead, sanctions at Earl Marshal took a more positive form of a short removal from school to work alongside community groups.

Chris Searle had already displayed an ability to link the powerless with people who could enable them to reach a wider audience. As head he also stimulated a remarkable process of interconnection among the school children. In

1992 the pupils at Earl Marshal organised support for the people of Guyana during a cholera epidemic, earning the thanks of the socialist president, Cheddi Jagan. Two years later a group of girls from Pakistani families decided to start a breakfast programme to make sure all the children ate before school. And when boys of Pakistani and Somali descent were in conflict, the boys from Yemeni families told their head not to worry. Their diplomatic intervention secured peace.

The values of Sheffield Education Committee shifted and regardless of protest by Tony Benn and other left Labour MPs, Chris Searle lost his job. He taught English to retired Yemeni steelworkers who had faced danger and racism when they left their farms for Sheffield's Attercliffe in the 1950s and 1960s. Then he became a visiting professor at the University of York in Toronto. It was a home from home for the wandering poet-scholar who found that 'everyone from everywhere was there'. He settled in happily with his cosmopolitan students and introduced poems by children of Sheffield immigrant families to Canadian Mohawk children in voluntary classes at a reservation school.

Chris Searle's memoirs can be read for the stories, but they also remind us that 'education' comes from a word meaning 'to draw out' rather than pumping in and measuring by slide rule. His life is a challenge to all those repressive mind manacles imposed by the Conservatives in the 1980s and which have accrued ever since.

Along the way he also tells us about many aspects of radical culture, from the journal *Artery* to centres like the Half Moon Theatre in East London and the Garage in the West. He describes small black community publishing initiatives like Karia and writers like Peter Blackman from Barbados – poet, railway fitter and friend of Paul Robeson, and the editor of *Race and Class* from Sri Lanka, A. Sivanandan.

During the 2000s Chris Searle became Director of Ahmed Iqbal Ullah Race Relations Centre at Manchester University. There he continued to add his voice against many kinds of injustice and, yet again, went around schools, stimulating and gathering poems, this time in celebration of Nelson Mandela's 90th birthday in 2008. They were published in *Mandela, Manchester* in 2009.

He was also to be found in the anti-racist cricket movement, Hit Racism for Six, along with the socialist political thinker, Mike Marqusee, as well as supporting a group of Manchester United Football Club members who started Let's Kick Racism Out of Football in the city. I remember them fondly as an imposing lot who kindly appointed themselves as informal bodyguards at the 'Sources of Radicalism' meetings I helped to organise through Manchester University's Labour Studies Group in the 1990s.

Pick up *The World is in Our Words* and be enthused by energy unbounded, going in several directions at once. But what, I wondered as I read, does this man do to relax? He gives us no clues. So I imagined him spinning words as he bowls and composing lines of poetry while fielding at third man or some deep cover point.

Sheila Rowbotham

Preface

What follows is the second part of an autobiography. The first part, *Isaac and I* told of my life and my involvement in poetry and education until 1976 when I went to Africa to teach in Mozambique. This second part begins in 1979 and continues until the beginning of 2020, when it was written in Sheffield, during the lockdown caused by the coronavirus pandemic.

I deliberately have not included the two years I spent teaching secondary school students and adults in Mozambique between 1976 and 1978, or a further two years between 1980 and 1982 when I was teaching unqualified young teachers in revolutionary Grenada. Those experiences are set down in *'We're Building the New School!' Diary of a Teacher in Mozambique* and *Grenada Morning: a memoir of the Revo*.

I have subtitled both parts of my autobiography *A Life in Poetry*, because poetry and its stories and words have always been an essential part of my life as a teacher, and the means that I have used to speak and forge imaginative empathy amongst the people I have taught from primary and secondary school children in London, Yorkshire, Tobago, Mozambique and Manchester to working adults in Africa and Canada and veteran ex-steel workers in Sheffield. For me, education and poetry are the flesh and blood of the same striving for human betterment, and I remember my old Sri Lankan friend Siva writing in his introduction to my book *Living Community, Living School* that education itself is the power that 'elicits every conceivable possibility of the human mind and soul', and that our children are truly 'the measure of our possibilities'.

When I look back over my life in education and poetry over fifty years, in three continents, I can see a life sometimes of lost causes, but losses which are part of a greater trajectory towards betterment and freedom. I was sacked

11

from my London school in 1971, yet my students' support and the loyalty of my union meant I was reinstated with the brilliance of children's creative writing vindicated and strengthened. My time in Mozambique taught me how a school could be transformed by revolutionary principles, even though that young nation attacked by an apartheid neighbour, civil war and neo-liberal economies, has put aside the principles that won it its independence. I gave everything I had to the Grenada Revolution, helped to train its teachers, develop its publishing and democratise its budget, but saw such a crucial and influential process crack apart and implode in factionalism and deadly violence. Yet the memory of its successes and transformations will not die, throughout the Caribbean, and in small island states everywhere. The work done in tackling racism and exclusion in Sheffield schools, despite my own exclusion in helping to promote it, made significant steps forward in the city that will not be for nothing. Out of loss comes hope and the promise of change. If life has taught me anything it has taught me this: that with struggle, perseverance, imagination and optimism, there will be a new and more just day for all of us, the ordinary and working people of our world. And if now-times tells us the truth of the world, it is those people with their brainpower, intense courage and loyalty to other human beings like themselves: our doctors, nurses, cleaners, health workers, carers for the sick and the old, transport workers, shop workers, garbage workers, farm and factory workers, teachers, cleaners, those who produce our food, clothes and energy, who every day sustain our lives and work to make them better. They are the true makers and poets of our world.

And one last small victory which I know I can share with young people all over the world, whose consciousness and activism provoked it. On March 29, 2020, on the streets of Minneapolis, USA, a black Texan named George Floyd was murdered by police as their knees squeezed his neck and suffocated him despite his last imploring words to them: 'I can't breathe!' The worldwide anti-racist response to this brutal crime was unprecedented; all over the world young people took to the streets in repugnance and protest – in London and Bristol too, where statues of slaveowners and slavery profiteers were torn down in anger. In Stepney, East London, where I had been dismissed from my teaching post in 1971, at the Sir John Cass and Redcoat Church of England Secondary School, the governors of the school decided to dispense with its name. Cass was discovered to have been a major profiteer of the eighteenth century slave trade and a leading member of the Royal African Company which traded in slaves with most of its investors' funds used to hire slave ships – complete with their Church of England blessing – plying between West Africa and Virginia and the Caribbean.

Generations of East London children at the school endured the annual Founder's Day Service in the St. Botoph's Church, Aldgate in the City of London, which they were compelled to attend while wearing red feathers in obeisance to Cass. The legend was that he had died coughing up blood, staining the white feathers of his quill pen red, as he signed away a portion of his slave-trading riches to found the school.

Cass's name had also been dropped with his bust removed from the Guildhall in the City, and the City of London Corporation saying that it symbolised 'a stain on our history'. It was strange, yet heartening for me and many others, pupils, teachers and all, to read this. Half a century before, I had written a poem about Sir John Cass, which had been published as part of an appendix to my book, *This New Season*. Its final verse was this:

So now you youth all through this land
Don't do your masters' duty.
Take the new world by the hand
And carve your own fresh beauty!

All caused by the death of a black man in Minneapolis, USA: how small is our world, how interconnected are its people.

13

So despite the present human tragedy everywhere around us, I dedicate this book to every student that I have ever taught, from infants to veterans, no matter where or when, and to the precious future of their own children and grandchildren and the world in which they will live, struggle and thrive.

Chris Searle, 2022

Chapter 1
Moonlight and Sunflowers

After I came back from Nampula in Mozambique in November 1978, I quickly found a teaching post at my old school, Langdon Park in Poplar, East London, and set about trying to strengthen solidarity between teachers in Britain with teachers in Mozambique. I spoke about the revolutionary changes within the education system and the 'New Schools' in Mozambique at a large-scale meeting at the Africa Centre in Covent Garden. The meeting was full with many London teachers and Africans eager to know about progress in Mozambique, from Ghana, Nigeria, those exiled from South Africa and Zimbabwe, from where squads of Ian Smith's Rhodesian army were still attacking Mozambican villages over the frontier. I started off the meeting by teaching the listeners the children's song *A Escola Organizada* with its simple Portuguese words. The assembly joined in heartily, and there, in the midst of London's West End, the words direct from revolutionary Africa boomed out over the fruit market, the theatres, pubs and restaurants. The atmosphere was radiating support and the only sour moment was when one young white man, with a sheaf of ultra-leftist newspapers on his lap, disputed that there could ever be a socialist revolution in Mozambique or Africa generally because it had little or no working class. His assertion caused indignation and uproar particularly from Africans, and his doctrinaire arguments were angrily rejected.

I had just returned from working in a school in liberated Africa that was transforming itself from a colonial, racist and Eurocentric institution with an imperial curriculum and a Catholic-based, authoritarian structure, to a new breed of school, following a pathway of complete democratic

15

change with a new peasant and worker-based student population, and on-the-job, emergency-trained young teachers full of militant ideals to reach the mass of the people. During daytime classes I had taught teenagers from surrounding impoverished suburbs and villages; during the evening local workers and women setting themselves free from drudgery and male domination, all determined to learn English as a vital international language, both throughout their continent and throughout the world. In the future I was to set the details of all this down in my book *'We're Building the New School!': Diary of a Teacher in Mozambique*, generously introduced by one of my writer-heroes, the scholar-activist Basil Davidson. Davidson had worked and reported from the frontline of the national liberation struggles of Frelimo in Mozambique, the PAIGC led by Amilcar Cabral in Guinea-Bissau, and the MPLA in Angola in perhaps his finest book *In the Eye of the Storm,* where he had been side-by-side with the movement's remarkable leader and poet, Agostinho Neto.

But the publication of that account was a few months on, and it was Liberation, formerly the Movement for Colonial Freedom, that gave me tremendous support in organising events and publishing materials which showed not only the courage and creativity of the Mozambican people, but also the progress being made in their youthful, independent nation. I was invited on to Liberation's Central Council, and I remember as a comparatively young member, how honoured and nervous I felt in the company of such veteran campaigners. All around me at the monthly meetings were people of a huge and often heroic mould. The President, Fenner Brockway, who had worked closely with Keir Hardie, had actively supported the suffragettes, been an early member of the Independent Labour Party, and been imprisoned for his socialist opposition to the First World War, finally being released in 1919. In 1929 he became MP for Leyton East, helped launch the League Against Imperialism, campaigned for the Spanish Republic and helped create the Movement for Colonial Freedom in 1954.

His support for national liberation movements encompassed the world: in India, Ghana, Kenya, Nigeria, and Vietnam. He was an early opponent of Apartheid and nuclear weapons (as a founder member of the Campaign for Nuclear Disarmament). I remember too Irishman Desmond Greaves, representing the Connolly Association and author of many fine books on Ireland, and the remarkable Jamaican Billy Strachan (1921–1998) who had been a wireless operator and air gunner on Wellington bombers as a 21 year old in 1941, then re-trained as a pilot at Cranwell, became a Flight Lieutenant and had flown Lancasters. Staying in Britain, he became an anti-racist and anti-imperialist lawyer and campaigner in the post war years. There was Joan McMichael, doctor campaigner, author and organiser of Medical Aid for Vietnam. I very soon became a close friend of Liberation's General Secretary, the tiny Tony Gilbert, born in Poplar in 1914 and ex-furrier, Yorkshire miner, International Brigadier and survivor of the Spanish Civil War, railway shunter and National Union of Railwaymen militant, and his ever-busy, ultra-dedicated partner Kay Beauchamp who had been International Secretary of the Communist Party and one of the founders of the *Daily Worker* in 1930.

In early 1977 I had been one of the very few white

Kay Beauchamp, a
Daily Worker founder,
died in January 1992
aged 91.

people present at the huge public meeting addressed by Samora Machel, President of Mozambique, at Nampula football stadium. Nampula is the largest city in the north of the country – an ex-garrison city from where the Portuguese colonial army had waged its war against the Frelimo guerrillas who had created liberated areas in the northern provinces of Niassa and Cabo Delgado. One of the President's themes in his

17

Chris Searle with
Tony Gilbert 1980.

animated speech – delivered like a true African story-teller,
full of gesticulation, foot movement, striding up and down
with exaggerated grimaces, laughs and exclamations, was
about how much colonial racism had set out to warp the
consciousness of Africa's colonized peoples. Many of his sentences brought back Fanon to my mind, but it was when he
began to emphasise the power of internationalism and the
signal truth of class that I found myself totally drawn
inside his words. 'It is Portuguese colonialism and fascism
that were our enemies,' he declared, 'not the Portuguese
people! The working people everywhere are our friends. It
doesn't matter whether they are white or black. If they help
us, they are our friends, no matter where they come from.'
I had already met and begun to work with white ex-

18

Portuguese, now Mozambican teaching colleagues, with colleagues from Tanzania, South Africa, Guinea and Zimbabwe, as well as Belgian, Dutch, Canadian, Bulgarian, and Cuban doctors and health workers and sensed the power of internationalism all around me.

Machel's speech stayed in my head and in my blood, and one of my first writing tasks when I returned to London was to write a short account, which I called *Beyond the Skin*, explaining and exemplifying the Mozambican commitment to anti-racism. When I showed it it Liberation comrades, they wanted to publish it and its designer, Nick Wright, photogaphed a thematic Makonde sculpture that I had brought home with me, portraying a Portuguese colonial administrator carried in a chair by two African servants, while vassal African troops beat their own countrymen with batons and a *palmatoria* – the name given to a hard wooden block carved to inflict pain and bruising on the open hands of its victims. The pamphlet also included a number of poems written in English by my students, including this one by sixteen year old José Maria de Carlos

The Worker Yesterday

Dawn...
The worker thinks
thinks of the whip
Dawn...
The worker thinks
thinks of the dust in the mines
  Dawn...
The worker thinks
thinks he is capable
  Dawn...
Now the worker
thinks of the communal tasks.

I had begun the account with a Machel quotation:

Racism, whether it is whites in relation to blacks, or blacks in relation to whites, is one of the most degrading and humiliating forms of the system of the exploitation of man

by man, the instrument preferred by the reactionary classes
to divide, isolate and wipe out progressive forces...

The complexes which are manifested express the weight of
the old mentality which we still carry inside us. The strug-
gle for us to destroy this inheritance is one of the essential
moments of creating the new mentality.

In his preface to the pamphlet, Stan Newens, then Labour MP for Harlow and Chair of Liberation, emphasised that 'it has many lessons for us in Britain; and sees a future free of racism, a future in which development of the full potential of people will be what life is about'. While Mozambique's southern neighbour was still ruled by Apartheid, and Rhodesia to its west was still stricken by the racist Smith regime which launched regular deadly attacks on Mozambique and its people, here was a nation showing the world how to tackle one of the century's most rampant. and inhuman deformities.

Meanwhile, I was back in Langdon Park School, Poplar, teaching English again in my old classroom. It was as if I'd never left. In my new classes I found sisters and brothers of some of my former students and a similar keenness to learn, imagine and create in words. In December 1979, a West Indian youth Michael Ferreira, born in Stanleytown, Guyana, now living in Hackney, had been attacked and stabbed by a racist gang as he walked home one night with some friends. Badly wounded, he had been taken into Stoke Newington Police Station, where Michael's friends had asked the officers at reception to phone straight away for an ambulance. The police had delayed the call, taking invaluable time by launching accusative questions at the black youths, and eventually Michael had died from his wounds on the way to the hospital. There was large scale community outrage right across East London. At Michael's funeral procession I walked with Blair Peach, whom I hadn't seen for two years, and he told me about his own struggles over those years, including being targeted by both the police and members of the National Front on the streets of East London. I would meet Blair regularly on Sunday mornings at Brick Lane Market, where activists of the Tower Hamlets Movement Against Racism and Fascism (THMARF) mounted a bookstall to counteract local groups of National Front selling their newspaper.

Back at school, my class of fourteen-year-olds wrote a play collectively about Michael's death. The class were divided into five groups and each group wrote a scene with a particularly conscious Mauritian boy writing a prologue, which began:

The evil wings of racism have once again spread over this country,
The evil that has brought fear -
and I warn my black brothers
if they see or hear racism -
Stay clear!

I went to visit Michael's mother and showed her the play, interviewing her about her son's life, and asked her permission to publish the students' work. She agreed, so we brought it out as a pamphlet, encouraging other teachers to do similar work in their classes. The dramatist Edward Bond wrote to me about the play: 'It's a very raw, disturbing piece – with the child's photographic eye for the truth'. I could have written something similar about his own plays, so deeply had they impacted upon me. The short play had a stimulating effect across the school when we read it in the classroom. I was regularly taking thirteen- and fourteen-year-old students to the Theatre Royal, Stratford and two boys in my class were particularly impressed by Trinidadian Mustapha Matura's play, *Welcome Home, Jacko*, with its powerful Caribbean-London language and magnetic characters. Sean, a white boy from the grim Coventry Cross Estate in Bow, living in straitened circumstances with his single mother and younger siblings, and Paul from a Jamaican family in Mile End, wrote a play together about the formation of an anti-racist group. They called the group and the play *Moonlight,* emulating Matura's grasp of realistic Caribbean dialogue. Here's how the name *Moonlight* becomes chosen by the boys:

Ray: Well, first we have to think of a name for us
Markus: 'ow 'bout 'DREADS AGAIN' RACISM'?
Fritzroy: Nah man, we call it MOONLIGHT.
Ray: Why 'MOONLIGHT'?
Fritzroy: Ya know dat chocolate called Moonlight, wid de half milk, half plain chocolates?
Ray: Yeah, I like that! I think that would be just right.
Jahvah: Nah man, you can't have a name like dat.
Ray: Why not?
Jahvah: 'cause it does sound stupid?
Fritzroy: Ey man, yah is calling I suggestion stupid?
Jahvah: Yea?
Fritzroy: Well den, ya come up wid a better one.

They have a vote and *Moonlight* is adopted. We filmed the play, which was later published by the Inner London Education Authority's English Centre and distributed widely across the city's schools. On a later visit to the Theatre Royal we went to see another Matura play, *Nice*, with its lone character sweeping out a canteen and reflecting upon his life in a long monologue. At the play's end it is revealed that he has been sweeping a prison canteen. Portrayed by the brilliant Guyana-born actor Norman Beaton who was later to play the main character in the television series *Desmond's* set in a Caribbean London barber's, Beaton also played Lord Byron in Adrian Mitchell's play on Blake, *Tyger,* which I had seen with my students seven years before. I sent a copy of *Moonlight* to Beaton who invited the two young playwrights to his Theatre

Royal dressing room telling them how impressed he was with their writing, cracking jokes, telling stories and offering good advice and encouraging them to 'keep on keeping on'. They did exactly that. Paul qualified as a lawyer and worked for the Crown Prosecution Service. He told me in April 2020: 'The backstage visit to Norman Beaton's dressing room is something I will never forget. Given all his success, I will never forget his warmth and way he welcomed two East End boys with his encouragement; a great actor and also a great human being. I remember how much I laughed during that incredible one-man performance. Especially his opening line 'When I came off the boat.' It had a special impact on me. It was something I had often heard my Dad say when he was to embark on another of his monologues.'

As for Sean, after working as a builder's labourer and other manual jobs, he eventually qualified as a teacher and later gained a doctorate, also writing a book setting out his educational ideas and published under the title *Living Contradictions: A Teacher's Examination of Tension and Disruption in Schools, in Classrooms and in Self*. He told me 'I had a sense of awe, being mesmerised by him standing alone on that stage with only a broom – quite something for an impressionable fourteen-year-old. He also imparted a gift by way of a simple and understated, yet profound bit of advice: 'Keep on keeping on''. It encapsulates my memory of a cherished time with my childhood pals at Langdon Park School'.

Certainly, their creative determination inspired me too as I took another idea to Liberation. This was the genesis of *Young World Books*, an idea to create a series of books aimed at young people in British classrooms. In 1978 there were few books for British school students which focused on the experiences and struggles of the new, decolonised nations and those still involved in confronting the power of Eurocentricity and colonial racism in Africa, the Caribbean and Latin America. Although there was the beginning of a burgeoning of novels, stories and poetry reflecting the

23

multi-racial truth of London schools, some of this was less about true life and racist reality than the more nebulous, multicultural ideals of 'steel-bands and samosas'. As *Young World Books* set out in its manifesto: 'Our classrooms have become microcosms of the world. A new reality of a young world of developing nations has challenged the Eurocentricity of our educational syllabus. British schools can no longer afford to isolate themselves from this new consciousness. The old racist, parochial and narrow outlook on the rest of the world and its peoples which characterised British imperial education needs to disappear along with the colonial flags which have been lowered forever in the de-colonised world. Too few of the books available to our schools actually make clear, without apology or nostalgia, an anti-imperial attitude. *Young World Books* seeks to make this message clear.'

Liberation's response was full of enthusiasm, particularly from Kay Beauchamp and Tony Gilbert. We managed to get a founding grant from the Rowntree Trust and then choose the first title of the imprint: *Tales of Mozambique.* I had read and translated the simple Portuguese of these animal fables, human stories, allegories and realistic, sometimes brutal oral folk tales, mainly from the popular paperback *Contos Mocambicanos,* during my second year in Nampula. My Portuguese was never strong, but I could just about manage translating these stories. I had got to know in London two brilliant young art students – Chaz Davies of Zimbabwe and Ruhi Hamid of Tanzania – who took on the tasks of book design and illustrating each story. They contacted eighteen of their friends, co-students and tutors and with a powerfully creative collection of drawings in a compendium of styles, moods, humour and pathos, they designed a black and white, lavishly illustrated A4-size collection which is truly the most visually stimulating book I have ever been associated with. The artists came from Australia, Ireland, Thailand, Ecuador, Sri Lanka, India, USA, South Africa, Hong Kong, Italy, Ghana and England. The book was launched at a 'Viva Mozambique' solidarity event for Mozambique at the Africa Centre, with African food and music from an internationalist array of performers including the Trinbago Dancers, the Caribbean baritone James Phillips who sang like Paul Robeson, US protest folksinger Jack Warshaw and another future character of *Desmond's*, (this time Porkpie) – the Guyanese singer and actor Ram John Holder, whose pioneering album *Black London Blues* had been released in 1969 and is full of humour, anger and satirical edge. It was a memorable night.

Our second book was from Angola, *Ngunga's Adventures,* written by Pepetela, the pseudonym of Artur Pestana, who became Vice-minister of Education in the MPLA government. Written in simple and deeply moving poetical Portuguese, it tells the story of Ngunga, a young war orphan. As he travels through his nation's war zones, trying to find a world where people think less about themselves and more about each other, he experiences cruelty, love, despair and courage – particularly that of his teacher, Union. He begins to understand the adult word of exploitation and struggle, recognising too that he is involved in his people's fight for freedom and independence – and he sets his mind upon leaving a way of life where his people's minds as well as their bodies are trapped behind the barbed wire. Translated by me and illustrated by a young English art student, Steve Lee who had been one of the artists of *Tales of Mozambique,* it became a much-read novel in Britain and Africa. Pepetela, in giving permission for us to publish his work, suggested that copies should be sent to those young people in struggling nations like Zimbabwe, Namibia and South Africa by a 'Buy a Book for Africa' campaign, whereby those buying the book in Britain could also buy an extra copy which could be sent to school students across Africa. After the independence of Zimbabwe in April 1980, *Ngunga's Adventures* became one of the essential books of the new nation's national curriculum.

It was launched at the first of two such events in a committee room in the House of Commons. Kay Beauchamp described the launch in the January 1981 issue of the journal *Liberation*, with my old student Paul Parris, co-author of *Moonlight*, well involved:

> A splendid, if unusual event took place at the House of Commons on December 15.
>
> With Dennis Canavan MP in the chair, Neil Kinnock MP (Labour's spokesman on Education) warmly welcomed the publication of such books as *Tales of Mozambique* and *Ngunga's Adventures* by Young World Books and sponsored by Liberation.
>
> "They should," he said, "be a part of the syllabus of every school. They could play as vital part in promoting understanding of our multi- cultural society as *The Diary of Anne Frank* achieved in exposing fascism in Germany."
>
> The audience were in for some special treats – Paul Parris, a fifteen-year-old Black Briton, read extracts from *Ngunga*

Authors of
Moonlight,
Sean Warren
and Paul
Parris.

with great feeling and he expressed his love for such literature. He had previously read stories from *Tales of Mozambique* on BBC's radio programme "Black Londoners". The House of Commons has special rules so no music is allowed. Perhaps it was just as well for we discovered new talent from folk singer Ram John Holder.

As part of his welcome to Young World Books he came prepared to sing but instead he read his own poems from the Caribbean. They were splendid, and as Neil Kinnock said, "Change the location and their message applies to Britain and the problems this Tory Government is heaping on our people."

Pepetela's novel certainly had a deep effect on some of my students as we read it in the classroom. Brian, whose parents had been born in St Vincent, wrote this poem dedicated to its young protagonist:

Free the People, Ngunga

Ngunga was a brave comrade
Fighting for his country,
Freeing his people from their slavery,

27

Fighting for hospitals for its people,
Fighting for his people to read and write,
Fighting for his people to have full bellies,
Fighting for his women to be free,
Fighting for his brothers and sisters all over Africa –
   Their country!
Fighting to make Africa the most beautiful place in the world.
Free the people, Ngunga!

We also published the first young people's collection of short stories and poems from revolutionary Cuba, including work by poet Nicolas Guillen and an especially moving short story from Samuel Feijoo called *Private Eloi*. Young World Books were beginning to find favour, particularly among London teachers, and the resource centres created by the Inner London Education Authority which were often administered by progressive ex-teachers with strong internationalist attitudes, were stocking and promoting them.

Illustrated by Steve Lee

***

In April 1979, Blair Peach, was killed by the Special Patrol Group of the Metropolitan Police during an anti-National Front street demonstration in Southall, West London, where a strongly organised Asian community had protested and resisted the interlopers' attack on their neighbourhood. In the *London Evening News* of 24 April, a close witness, Mr Parminder Atwal, described Blair's fatal encounter with about twenty police, running towards him when he was alone, carrying shields and black truncheons:

> As the police rushed past him, one of them hit him on the head with the stick. I was in my garden and saw this quite

clearly. When they all rushed past he was left sitting against the wall. He tried to get up, but he was shivering and looked very strange. He couldn't stand. Then the Police came back and told him like this: 'Move! Come on, move!' They were very rough with him and I was shocked because it was clear he was seriously hurt.

His tongue seemed stuck in the top of his mouth and his eyes were rolled up back to the top of his head. But they started pushing him and told him to move, and he managed to get to his feet. He staggered across the road and came to where I was in the garden. I tried to sit him down. He was in a very bad state and he couldn't speak. Then he just dropped down. I got a glass of water for him, but he couldn't hold it and it dropped out of his hand.

I wasn't in Southall that afternoon. I somehow hadn't heard about the march. But when I heard on our kitchen portable radio the next morning that an East London teacher had been killed at the demonstration, even before his name was announced, I knew it was Blair, for he was the bravest, the most forthright and committed of all of us. In November 2019, some of his old trade union and school colleagues held a memorial meeting to him in Mile End Library, forty years after his death, for which no policeman has ever been prosecuted. A late middle-aged Asian man rose from the assembly and said, with a simple eloquence: 'Mr Peach was my teacher. He did everything for me and changed my life for the better, teaching and inspiring me. All my life, I will always remember him.'

***

I had become an editorial board member of the socialist art journal *Artery* and a friend of its dynamic editor, artist Jeff Sawtell, on my return from Mozambique. With very little money and few resources beyond the huge energy of its contributors and readers, *Artery* had not only kept going for nearly a decade, but published many articles on art and socialism from William Morris to Picasso, from Orozco and

29

the Mexican Mural Movement to Nazrul Islam and Bengali rebel poetry. As the journal's makers made clear in its prefacing principles: '*Artery* features work from all over the capitalist world, the socialist world, the liberated 'Third World' and those fighting against imperialism, both practical and theoretical. *Artery* encourages all those active in the struggle for socialism, world peace and international friendship.' These were founding principles which certainly chimed with me, and over the *Artery* years I wrote many reviews, articles and poems for the journal.

Editorial board members also talked earnestly about how we could create an organisation that would seek to unite and organise many genres of artists against the advancing threat of racism and fascism across Britain, and the growth, in particular of the National Front. We decided to create a movement, which we called Art Against Racism and Fascism, and I agreed to do my best to set up a group of poets. It isn't always easy to organise artists of any description particularly when many are geared to individualism and sometimes a cellular view of the world, but when I called a meeting of prospective poet-members of a 'Writers' sub-section' at the Half Moon Theatre in Alie Street, Stepney, the response was very positive and many came one July night in 1979, determined to add their creative weight. Michael Rosen read his poem *Fighters for Life* and Peter Blackman, the Barbadian poet and friend of Paul Robeson, read his beautifully moving internationalist anthem, with its long, long lines: *Stalingrad*. The dramatist Edward Bond had written some poems for the occasion including his hard-hitting *When the Right Took Power in England* and *The Art of the Audience*. The readings were followed by a discussion of the nature of the activities of such an organisation, which sought to unite professional and worker writers in many areas of creativity. A teacher from the Clissold Park School in Stoke Newington began by saying how essential it was to engage writers in school to stimulate work on anti-racism. Ken Worpole said that it was particularly important that local worker-writers be

30

involved in such work, attesting that writers' groups of the Federation of Worker Writers and Community Publishers were making such school interventions in many British cities, and that they would be an invaluable ally in promoting such work. There was much discussion about combining the talents and commitment of both professional writers and worker writers, and the importance of engaging trade unions too in this work, and urging them to encourage and fund such initiatives taken by their members. Michael Rosen talked about the essential role of radio, and how anti-racist writers need to organise to ensure that their voices were continually heard on the airwaves.

Art Against Racism and Fascism began to engage and activate many creative people. There were other readings at the Half Moon, but the involvement of Gerald Chapman, the young director of the Royal Court Young People's Theatre was precious. He offered his venue, 'The Garage' close to Sloane Square, as a venue for events and was generous with both his time and resources. We held many events there. The African-American actor Joseph Mydell put on his one-man show on the life of the poet Paul Lawrence Dunbar; we held a Jazz Against Racism mini-concert, featuring the great free soprano saxophonist Lol Coxhill, who often busked on Waterloo Bridge, and a quartet led by alto saxophonist Bruce Turner, with pianist Michael Garrick, bassist Dave Green and drummer Alan Jackson. The audience was grooving that night. I remember another powerful reading by poet Adrian Mitchell and stand-up comedy by Alexei Sayle and Bill Monks. There was also a performance by Ewan McColl and Peggy Seeger, and a memorable evening by Blackman, who read *Stalingrad* then spoke with a powerful eloquence about poetry, racism and internationalism. Sitting in the audience was the ex-drummer of the Soft Machine, Robert Wyatt and his partner, the artist Alfie Benj, together with one of my absolute heroes, the film actress of *Billy Liar*, *Darling*, *Doctor Zhivago* and *Far from*

SONGS AND POEMS from EAST END TRADE UNIONS
Bengali Musicians
BISHRI
with Singer
ABDUS SALIQUE

Alfie Benj's leaflet.

the Madding Crowd – Julie Christie. It turned out to be her fortieth birthday, and at the end of the evening we all sat in a Sloane Square pub and celebrated it with her. I was sitting next to Robert, who was deeply moved by Peter Blackman's rendition of his *Stalingrad* poem. He asked him whether he could put his reading on the flipside of his next record. Peter was pleased to oblige, so AARF started getting into the charts!

I used to visit the remarkable Blackman regularly in his Belsize Park basement flat, where we would talk about politics and poetry and he would tell me about his stonemason father (who died when he was two) and his laundress mother from Barbados, and how the Anglican Church sent him to Durham University to train for the priesthood, and how as a priest he was sent to Gambia before the war. He soon discovered that the Church of England was paying a higher stipend to white priests than to their black counterparts, the cause of his resignation and return to London. He told me about his years in the Communist Party and as a steam engine mechanic in the Willesden railway works as the only railway fitter who could speak Greek and Latin. His Whitmanesque poem, *My Song is for All Men* was published just after the war to international acclaim, and he formed a strong friendship with Paul Robeson, who would stay at his family home in Hampstead (very close to the house where John Keats lived) and leave all the gifts he was given on his international singing tours in the Blackman family care. As I write this, on the wall opposite my desk is a photograph of Blackman, Robeson and W.E.B. Dubois greeting each other at the Paris World Peace Conference in 1949.

In 2012 I asked Robert Wyatt why Blackman's readings of his poetry had such a profound effect upon him all those years before. 'At a time of dramatically anti-establishment gestures,' he told me, 'his quiet, undemonstrative dignity as he crystallised key moments in our collective history, was a heartwarming revelation.' Then I heard from another old friend, Danny Reilly, who had worked alongside him 40 years before at Willesden and had suddenly discovered his history and stature as he sought to sell him a leftwing newspaper: The story seemed to exemplify Blackman's principles in life and poetry of 'excellence in the ordinary'. Danny told me: "I met Peter Blackman over forty years ago, when he was my age now. It was by accident, at Willesden Junction railway yard where we both worked. I remember I offered to sell him a socialist newspaper, interrupting him getting changed, and was silenced with surprise by both the tone and content of his reply. 'Marxism I have always considered superior to bourgeois liberalism,' he began. His accent was both BBC English and West Indian. Nobody in our yard spoke like that, did they? He was a living contradiction – a political philosopher and a black railway worker. Only several years later did I discover who it was who had so politely declined my invitation to 'buy a paper mate', and gone on to give me a brief education in socialist politics. Unknown to me, and most of the left then, Peter Blackman had been a Caribbean left wing activist and poet since he was 28, when in 1937, he had moved from Barbados to live in Britain. He became a leading activist and writer working in a range of organisations: the Negro Welfare Association, the League of Coloured Peoples, the Committee for West Indian Affairs, the League Against Imperialism. During the Second World War, turned down from the armed forces, he worked assembling Wellington bombers. I had no idea back in 1970 who this self-effacing railway worker was."

So now AARF had two reliable performance venues: The Garage up West and the Half Moon down East. In December 1980 we sought to put some creative strength behind the South East Region's Trade Union Congress to unionise the predominantly Asian workers in the clothing factories of Whitechapel and Spitalfields. Alfie drew a delicately beautiful poster of an Asian girl and white boy dancing, their scarves fluttering. We had a good turn-out and poems from East London trade unionists, the Bengali musicians Bishri and the singer Abdus Sabor performed, as did poets and singers Michael Rosen, Sandra Kerr, Jack Warshaw, and Arthur Clegg, who made friends all round with his poem **The English – Are they Human?**

I'm Celtic and Saxon, a Norman, a Dane
a bronze smith from Africa, India, Spain
a megalith mason
from the Middle Sea basin.
Continents, oceans
and wonderful notions
mix in my structure and seethe in each vein .

Forebears from Asia who tamed the wild horse,
slaves for my ancestor, Roman and Norse,
a Frenchman, a Fleming
Dutch, from Terschelling
Slavonic from Lublin
African seamen who served under Nelson,

Jew, Czechs and others fleeing from Belsen
descendant of legion from every region,
a myriad mixture – English, of course.

When Robert heard Bishri singing their stirring song in Bengali, *Trade Union*, he put that on a flipside too, making the song the toast of Brick Lane shops and restaurants. We began to think that we were getting somewhere.

Sometime in 1980, in the wake of the publication of *Beyond the Skin*, I was invited to the Institute of Race Relations, at their Pentonville Road HQ, for a discussion. It was an informal encounter, a round-the-table exchange with a number of powerful, mainly black activists. The Institute had recently freed itself from the grip of reactionary, business-orientated and neo-liberal sponsors, and established a radical activist platform in support of black, anti-racist campaigns in Britain and anti-imperialist struggles abroad, led by its director, the Sri Lankan ex-librarian and writer, A. Sivanandan. Its journal, *Race & Class* edited by Siva (as everybody knew him) and managed, composed and put together by two remarkable Englishwomen, Jenny Bourne and Hazel Waters, was a powerful vehicle of scholarly anti-racist and anti-imperialist messaging, with an editorial committee which included some outstanding scholars from Cedric Robinson to Basil Davidson, Hermione Harris and Thomas Hodgkin to Eqbal Ahmad and Colin Prescod. I hadn't for long been back from Mozambique, *Beyond the Skin* was circulating and I had no idea what to expect at the Institute meeting. As it turned out, I was battered. I was accused of simplistically seeking to apply the Mozambican race reality to the entirely different situation in Britain. I replied that I saw their point in the danger and folly of doing that, but it wasn't what I was seeking to do – particularly in the pamphlet. I was trying to demonstrate how Mozambique, faced by Apartheid South Africa to its south and racist Rhodesia to its west, was creating a new form of anti-racist life in the very heart of the Africa storm, and how that could inspire the anti-racist

A. Sivanandan, Founding Editor of *Race & Class*.

A. Sivanandan
1923-2018

movement in Britain. In 2009, Jenny Bourne remembered the meeting:

> He cannot have had any idea of what he was walking into. Actually, given his zeal, he probably did not give it a thought. But I have never witnessed a more one-sided, heated, explosive battle of ideas than that afternoon. For Chris was not just confronted by IRR's director Sivanandan and Chair Colin Prescod, but a number of other leading black activists who happened to be there – one from a black power-influenced self-help group, one from a black breakaway from the Fourth International, one from a community defence campaign. One after another they told Chris nicely and not-so-nicely that the black experience in Britain was not what he took it to be, that anti-racist answers (that worked in Mozambique) could not

be neatly extrapolated to another country where conditions were quite other, that race and class did not slot happily into one another. Five or six booming, bombastic voices raised against him.

As I walked up to Kings Cross station after that meeting I felt both bruised and reflective, and I probably needed such an encounter to help me re-analyse and re-imagine many of my thoughts. They were right in their arguments of the mistakes of substituting one political reality for another. I didn't think I was doing that, but the meeting certainly helped me get to grips with the unique contours of my own country's age-old racism again. Perhaps I needed that. But strangely enough, when I returned a few weeks later to the Institute, I began to forge a close link with some of the same people who had given me such a rough ride that rocky afternoon. I struck up a friendship with Siva, our mutual love of poetry and cricket seemed to make a brotherhood between us which grew closely and strongly until he died in 2018 at the age of 94 – he even wrote an introduction to my book of 1996 *Living Community, Living School*. From 1980 I began to contribute regularly to *Race & Class* beginning with a series of lengthy interviews with the Minister of Finance of Grenada Bernard Coard; the leader of the Socialist League of Malawi (Lesoma), Attati Mpakati, who was assassinated by the Banda government in 1983; and the great Barbadian poet Edward Kamau Brathwaite. By 1983 I was invited onto the Editorial Advisory Committee. Since then I have made many friends at the Institute, worked with the brilliance of Hazel and Jenny's editorial skills for forty years and always valued the advice and knowledge of its professional staff. Danny Reilly and his wisdom, humour and eternal cups of tea; Liz Fekete with her sharpest and widest knowledge on British and European racism; Harmit Athwal and her evergreen hard work and cooperative spirit, Frances Webber's piercing legal insights and Chair Colin Prescod's huge breadth of understanding, activism, warmth and rebelliousness. I've been the luckiest of people to have shared it for four decades. The poem that I wrote to Siva is also a salute to all of them:

Hello Siva

'We are here because you were there'   A. Sivanandan

Hello Siva
I'm here again
because you were there.
Tamil boyo
global insighter
King's Cross joker
human of cosmos
ideas through prisms of resistance
storms of life and beauty
agonies and joys of history
all around the alleyways of Kings Cross Road –
here and there, race and class
met in our brain
to make the now and future.
Open the batting of struggle!
First change of strategy!
I'm there again
because you're here.

After Siva died in 2018 there was a crowded memorial meeting to him at Conway Hall, Red Lion Square. As I walked to the meeting through the square, past the expressive sculpture of Fenner Brockway, his left arm held high, I remembered that it was here that the young University of Warwick student, Kevin Gately, had been killed during an anti-racist demonstration against the National Front in June 1974. Under the watchwords above the stage, from Shakespeare: 'To thine own self be true', Polonius's pithy advice in Hamlet to his son Laertes, a succession of Siva's friends and admirers spoke out their tributes. I had this to say:

The first time that I met Siva was in 1973, I think, at the Institute's original Jermyn Street centre. He was warm, friendly, and full of jokes as he invariably was, teasing me about getting the sack from my East London school for publishing my students' poems in *Stepney Words* a couple of years before. Then suddenly he quoted T.S. Eliot at me – some lines from the Four Quartets. I remember exclaiming 'Hang on Siva, Eliot was an arch-reactionary, a bloody Tory!' As he answered: 'Ah, but the language, the words, just listen to them!'

The next time I saw him, it was at the old premises in Pentonville Road. This time he quoted Keats at me, from the 1817 letter to Benjamin Bailey: 'I am certain of nothing but the holiness of the heart's affections and the truth of the imagination. What the imagination seizes as Beauty must be truth.'

Ever since then, when I've read Siva I've been kidnapped by his use of the English language – how he harnessed this, the most formidable and powerful of English imperial institutions and turned its base, oppressive, linguistic metal into golden, figurative, revolutionary insights, using his huge imaginative reach. He was a poet of ideas, and he used metaphor to forge those ideas – all in a second language.

Take his titles, for they all emanate from that Keatsian imagination and the metaphors it creates, from poetical truth grounded in the real world. His longing for ideas of freedom for the world's struggling peoples was a hunger to him, 'a different hunger'; how we must use the insights of the past to inform the present and forge the future came the startling image, 'catching history on the wing'; how those who fight back, cooperatively and generously – in the hearts of our cities too are bonded as 'communities of resistance'; how we must never forget our mistakes and successes but always learn from them, for 'when memory dies' so does our ability to criticise, self-criticise and create a new life together; and how the urge to change is not only in our brains but in our heartsblood too, for 'the heart is where the battle is.'

And how new forms of imperial power stemming from the new technology can be grasped and wielded in our own struggles – those 'circuits of imperialism' can give us a current and a currency to also help to set us free.

Siva lived to see institutions and forms of the imperialism he had known on his Tamil and internationalist pulses, transformed by those it sought to suppress and dehumanise. None so symbolically and pictorially as by those who played the oldest of imperial games: cricket. And I remember vividly how he and I saw it happen in June 1984, on the television in the Institute's old place. By sheer coincidence I called in there as, on the final day of the Lord's test, Clive Lloyd's West Indians chased down 342 to win the match, thanks to Gordon Greenidge's double century. We watched the glory of his square-cutting and Siva was transported, shaking with jubilation and delight as he saw yet another arch-imperial emblem, the iconic sport he had known so intimately and played as a youth in Ceylon, taken over, commanded and transformed by brilliant black cricketers from the Caribbean islands.

More than anyone I have ever read – and alongside Fanon and James – Siva showed us how the forms and very language of imperialism, – if we can grasp them, reconstitute them and liberate them, can help to set us free, create new metaphors and realities of socialism, and help our children find freedom too. Long live his memory, his struggle, his humanity and his language – for they all belong to us, all of us.

***

In 1980, wandering around Soho, along the streets where Marx and Shelley had lived and where Blake had been born, I called at the cramped offices of the publisher Allison and Busby in Noel Street. I spoke to Margaret Busby, a young Ghanaian publisher who had published the works of many of my beloved Caribbean writers, from Barbadian George Lamming, Roy Heath of Guyana and the great Trinidadian, CLR. James. I told her that I had translated and compiled a selection of poems from the Mozambique Revolution, and was interested to know whether she might be interested in publishing them. She was enthusiastic about the idea, so I returned with the manuscript a few days later.

I had called the collection *The Sunflower of Hope* a phrase taken from the poem *Pray, Maria!* By Jose Craveirinha (1922–2003):

From hatred and the war of men,
from the raped mothers and daughters,
from the children dead with anaemia,
and from all those who rot in the dungeons,
the sunflower of hope grows in the world.

Jose Craveirinha in 1978.

There were thirteen poems by Craveirinha in the compilation as well as many others by his contemporaries and a generation of younger poets. I had visited him in his house in the Maputo suburb of Mafalala in July 1978 and he had been both warm and responsive, as well as deeply modest. In the sixties he had become an early supporter of Frelimo and was imprisoned in solitary confinement by PIDE, the Portuguese secret police, between 1965 and 1969. From 1982, eight years after Frelimo took power, Craveirinha became the first president of the Association of Mozambican writers and his poetry of the degradation of Portuguese colonial rule and his hope for the future of his nation continues to resonate in the minds of Mozambicans, as one of his continent's greatest poetical spirits.

The Sunflower of Hope was published in 1982. My proudest moment with the compilation happened later that year. I had been interviewing CLR James in Brixton, and before I left, we swapped books. He gave me a signed copy of *Nkrumah and the Ghana Revolution* one of his most undersung books, and I gave him *The Sunflower of Hope*. We said our goodbyes and I caught the tube back to my home in Leyton, East London. The next morning I received a telephone call from a very excited James. 'That poetry from Mozambique is some of the greatest poetry of the

Twentieth Century', he exclaimed, and I couldn't have asked for a more authoritative opinion. I never met him again, but his words through the wires across London that morning have never left me.

The last book I edited before I went to Grenada for two years in 1980 to work for the Grenada Revolution, was an anthology called *Bricklight*. It was all done in a bit of a rush before I left for the Caribbean and it consisted of poems born from East London in the two centuries of struggle of its people. It was subtitled, *Poems from the Labour Movement in East London*, and my old friend Dan Jones' cover showed generations of East Londoners with their banners outside the docks' walls – Chartists, Match-girls, dockers, transport workers, rag trade workers, suffragettes, anti-fascists among a host of campaigners and protesters. I had hurriedly compiled the anthology with the help of the National Museum of Labour History in Limehouse Town Hall, and was prompted towards the title *Bricklight* by my Jamaican friend Andrew Salkey's title, *Breaklight*, which he gave to his 1971 collection of Caribbean poetry, which sits proudly on the shelf behind me.

I had found many of the poems through my researches into Labour journals in the Tower Hamlets History Library at Mile End, and others had been sent to me over the years by relatives of the poets or their trade union comrades. Some of the poetical language was elaborately conceived, like the anonymous *May-Time in Canning Town*.

> The high wind speeds cloud-galleons o'er the sky,
> And sets the wherries dancing where the tide
> Rushes in sunlit splendour up the wide
> And foam-flecked spaces of the estuary:
> White washing flaps its sails in gardens gay:
> The Earth's a bride arrayed in streaming white:
> On hedgerow, blossoming tree and woodland height
> Her banners wave, and all the world's at play.

And even in Canning Town, where no white tree
Symbols the far-flung rapture of the Spring,
Some dream of beauty by the wind is stirred,
Some envy of the careless birds that wing
High o'er her smoke, some longing for a word
To break her evil spell and set her free.

And other words were cruelly simple and real, like these of
Joseph Leftwich's *The Tailor*.

Have you ever heard that a tailor was ill?
I mean a real tailor, who stitches until
He feels that the needle goes right through his head
And he crawls with his stitching away to his bed.

No, indeed not, for a tailor sits cross-legged like a Turk,
And he stitches, until he drops dead from his work.

And there were now-times poems of intense anger and
struggle, invoking the Bangladeshi martyrs murdered on
East London streets, such as Abdus Sabor's poem below:

At the Price of Blood

The door of memories
Your memories
Will remain forever open
Written in drops of your blood
And it will bring back the tide of your memories.

The day will return
Year after year
And the time when the sun sets
Will become bright
With the glow of your blood
Writ large on the horizon
And memories of you
KENNITH SINGH, ISHAQUE, ALTAB ALI

Condemned, heartless, cruel murder
Countless souls protest with full voices:
'Is this man's humanity?
Is this civilisation of the civilised age?'
When walking in the street

43

Sudden killing at the hands of the ferocious
KENNITH SINGH, ISHAQUE, ALTAB ALI

Mother Bengal
Mother Bengal
Mine is impatience, sadness and bereavement.
In processions
Countless voices protest, angry and saddened
Let injustice be over forever!
Let the stream of the blood of the innocents
Bring that about!
Let people unite in embraces of friendship!
KENNITH SINGH, ISHAQUE, ALTAB ALI

Those who spread hatred
In the streets and alleyways
In this circular game of racism -
To stop their tricks
Come, my mother's children
My brothers and sisters
Valiant ones
Let us assemble under the flag of unity!
KENNITH SINGH, ISHAQUE, ALTAB ALI

There were also plenty of poems from the Basement and from my classroom, which looked over the museum in Limehouse and the stone lantern of Hawksmoor's edifice, St. Anne's Church. In the anthology was one particular poem written by one of my students, thirteen-year-old Tracey about that very church. Our class visited the church and climbed up the steep stairs of the lantern during my last week at the school. It had a saddening effect on me and was a long goodbye. The interior of St. Anne's was virtually derelict, unkempt and sullied by the piles of dead pigeons behind the altar. As we climbed upwards and reached the lantern itself, we could look down over the Thames and the neighbourhoods where many of our students lived. Hawksmoor's stones and the labours of those who erected them moved me immensely. I think they touched Tracey too

St. Anne's
Church,
Limehouse.

As the misty morn clears
    St Anne's church lantern
    so lonely and bare,
    and not even the birds
    stay to say hello.
    Big wooden door
so damp and cold,
graves old and damp
black and white with age.

I wonder how long
before the leaves
    touch the crisp green
grassy land,
that was once trodden upon,
and wept on with tenderness
    and heartache?

On the trees
the bark begins to break off.
Everything has to die.

As I walk around the church
    I notice the difference.
    One side is
    dirty and polluted
    where only the restless lay.

The other side
is peaceful and quiet
where only the peaceful lay.

As I reach
the big iron gates I realise
how wonderful life is.

I read one grave
    saying:
    'Born 1866
    Died in 1867'
as I'm glad I'm alive
to be loved
and cared for.

As I walk out
of the gates,
    I look back
at the misty blue
    sky
above St. Anne's Church lantern.

Tracey's poem took me back a decade to *Stepney Words*, poems written in Stepney Churchyard and to Tony's poem about another Hawksmoor church, Christchurch in Spitalfields, very close to the young poet's home:

My Way

Around my way
There's a church with a steeple.
It's ever so high
It almost scrapes the sky.
It has a bell

With a priest
Talkng about hell.

Around my way
What a smell!

What was it about churches and churchyards and these young people? It was East London history etched out on their very doorsteps; stone lanterns, dizzying steeples, the dead and the living in the very heart of their lives, markers of the past, keys to continuance, oases of reflection.

As for *Bricklight,* it caused a stir and a lot of positive responses. The *East End News* reviewer wrote: 'Poems written by the known – Shelley, Blake, Hood, Morris, Rosenberg: and poems by the unknown – dockers, garment workers, office workers, railwaymen, tobacco workers, poems by pupils and students. They are songs, satires, laments, poems of survival and victory, of bitterness, poems that teach and explain; poems of struggle for a better world. There is no collection quite like this one – so local, yet so varied and intense in feeling.' And David Widgery, a local doctor and writer put it this way in *New Society*: 'As a slim volume published by the West Ham education offices in 1922 noted, 'The city needs its singers', and this is an important and inspiring collection of their songs.'

Chapter 2
Bethnal Green and Shirebrook

I returned home to London again in August 1982, after two years working in Grenada for the 'Revo'. I had found myself involved in a multitude of tasks, from teaching in and leading the ambitious National In-Service Teacher Education Programme; developing a national publishing house, Fedon Publishers, assisting with the mobilization of democratic forums to discuss the people's budget; helping with the writing of the Prime Minister Maurice Bishop's speeches and teaching political education classes. I had never worked so hard and never written so hard either. I edited the first five titles of Fedon Publishers. I wrote regular articles for the national newspaper, *The Free West Indian*, compiled a book detailing the many dimensions of destabilisation organised and put into effect by Reagan's regime and wrote an account, published in 1983 called *Words Unchained: Language and Revolution in Grenada* about the transformation of language provoked by revolutionary change in the small island state. Later, following the disastrous implosion and collapse of the 'Revo' in October 1983 and the US invasion, I collected Bishop's speeches which were published under the title of *In Nobody's Backyard* and, six years later, after giving me time to deal with the shock and trauma of the events of 1983, I wrote an autobiographical memoir called *Grenada Morning* introduced by Tony Benn MP.

When I returned to London, there was nothing for me this time at Langdon Park School. A National Union of Teachers Colleague at Daneford School, Bethnal Green, and a brilliant teacher of English, born in Doncaster, Barry

Pateman, managed to find me a job there, so I was soon back in an East London classroom again but not in very familiar circumstances. Daneford was an all boys school with a very hard reputation. It certainly wasn't easy. Half the boys were Bangladeshi teenagers from the newly arrived community to the south in Spitalfields and the Brick Lane corridor where Ron McCormick and I had published *Stepney Words in* 1971. This was a community under permanent attack and relatively closed in upon itself for defence and self-protection. Some boys came from families struggling in the use of English who worked in the local clothing and catering trades. They were also the target of frequent racist attacks by a resurgent National Front and other neo-fascist groups, with local youth like Altab Ali and Kennith Singh the victims of racist murder on the streets. Many of the white Daneford boys lived north of the school, in and around Hoxton where the National Front had become particularly strong. These two male, teenage constituencies met and learned about each other and the streets and world around them in the same classrooms, corridors and playgrounds. The school atmosphere was charged with subliminal suspicion, hostility and sometimes outright violence, which the teachers, almost all of them white except for a small number of Bangladeshi teaching assistants, had to learn how to deal with.

The headteacher, Mr Monte, was a warm and liberal-minded man with Jewish roots who did his best to promote trust and geniality. But in that environment it was a profoundly difficult task. The school needed an explicit and clear anti-racist policy and practice. The Labour controlled Inner London Education Authority was recommending all its schools to adopt such a policy but many headteachers and their senior managements throughout London were nervous about establishing curriculum approaches and school practices which actually manifested that. Instead many schools created what many London teachers called a 'steelband and samosa' superficial curriculum change, which took the apparently innocuous and gentle cultural aspects of 'multicultural' life, while ignoring the racism that was embedded at the very heart of school life and curricula.

This became especially evident to me during the school's response to the Eid Festival in 1983. The Head suggested that the school honoured the festival by holding a special Eid party for the Muslim students who were about half of the school. Non-Muslim students were not invited – for it was thought they would not know what to make of it and it might provoke hostile reactions amongst the Hoxton boys. The party went ahead, with large amounts of rice, curries and samosas. It was strange to gauge the reaction of the Muslim boys. The school had never done anything like this before and the boys certainly weren't used to seeing food characterised as 'theirs' on large plates and trestles one side of the school hall. And these were boys who were generally quiet, polite, friendly and almost always affable. Yet suddenly, with no given signal yet almost communally they began to pick up the samosas – some of them were quite large, and throw them like Frisbees all around the school hall, laughing almost joyously as they did so as if something had been released deep inside them. Very few of them were eaten, most of them flying in the air and dropping all over the floor. The head was aghast, shocked and bewildered. He looked around at the teachers who also seemed nonplussed. There was no hostility coming from the boys, only laughter and, it seemed, ridicule, that the school should attempt to do something like this, at this place, in this way. To me, watching it happen all around me, it seemed as if the boys were saying: "We didn't come here for samosas. We can have all that in our homes, with our families. We came here to learn and find equality and for you all to admonish and reject all the racism in the classrooms and the streets and all around us. That is what we expect from you, not samosas."

A few days after the Eid fiasco, a twelve year old boy called Kashim sat quietly at his desk and wrote this with not a samosa in heart or mind, but a consciousness of what was real all around him for his life and that of his family:

51

Our City

I live in London
Where racism turns to violence,
My family are struggling
When news comes of bills going up.
Where I live
The streets are dirty
With rubbish thrown out that is stinking.

The housing is bad
Because burglars could get in
And then we turn sad.
We are frightened to go out at night
Just in case we are hauled into a fight .

We wake up at dawn
And give a big yawn.
We've got to go to school through a dark tunnel
Where were sure there's got to be trouble.
We get most of the bullying in school
But there's nothing I could do.

When it gets dark
White bullies come out with dogs that bark.
With knives that glow in the dark,
We're sure we're going to be struck.

The weather is usually cloudy,
Sometimes it turns rainy.
During winter fuels are needed badly-
Prices of food go up day by day;
Which makes my simply enjoying life go away.

It was this poem and the sense of belonging infused within
its title, that urged me to compile a collection of school students' poems written from schools in many parts of London
which like Kashim, I called *Our City*. The Greater London
Council had decided to brand 1984 'The Year of Anti-
racism' in London so this anthology would be a
contribution. At Liberation we decided that Young World
Books would publish it, and I asked the Kenyan novelist
Ngugi wa Thiong'o, probably Africa's greatest writer, to add

an introduction. I had known Ngugi in Grenada, and arranged for him to come to an Education, Culture and Production conference which I was organising there in the sister island of Carriacou. We had spent a couple of warm days together, and now he was in London, as a writer-in-residence of Islington Council. Ngugi wrote from his own heart, and consciousness just like the young people whose words followed his. Perhaps he was thinking of Kashim's poem when he wrote:

Cover design:
Jan Flavell

> Reading these poems has opened my eyes to a London I had always simply seen as a big city where people from the four corners of the earth meet. The London that emerges from these poems is a city lived in by many human beings with tears and laughter, and terror and hope. It is full of people struggling against degrading living conditions, against pollution, against harsh conditions imposed on them by others, and above all against fascist and police terror. In fact, like the cinema of Charlie Chaplin there is in these poems a policeman always lurking somewhere in the corner, ready to pounce on those fleeing knives that glow in the dark, the victims of an all encompassing terror.
>
> I have enjoyed reading these poems. They have made me see London in a slightly different way. They have made me feel closer to London. And it is very heartening to see these young people, aged from 6 to 18, and coming from different parts of the city, from different schools and from different nationalities, united in their vision of a world in which human beings can be truly human, cooperating in creative friendship, instead of clawing at each other.

Another admirer of *Our City* and of Young World Books generally, (the first two titles, *Tales of Mozambique* and *Ngunga's Adventures* had won the prestigious 'Other Award' of the *Children's Books Bulletin*) was the new leader of the Labour Party and Liberation supporter, Neil Kinnock. He said in particular of the poems of *Our City*: 'They inspire us, they give us hope and life, they fire us. They give us that insight, that piercing view of our society that has been put in such a beautiful and proud way in this book'. He also agreed to speak at another launch of the anthology in the House of Commons, where the families of the young poets packed out the large room to hear them read their work. Since many of the poems were about family, this was entirely apt. Some of the Daneford boys were in the anthology with poems about their parents and grandparents. There was Richard:

My Mum the Dinner Lady

My mum is an ordinary woman
Working in a kitchen all week
From ten till three,
Standing over a hot stove
Working in intense heat
Then having the trouble of serving the kids,
Because they point and don't state clearly what they want.

Then the trouble of washing up!
When my mum comes home she's puffed out,
Then she has to start cooking again,
Then she has to wash up again
My mum can't wait till she gets to bed.

And Michael could only dream about his granddad:

My Grandfather in Cyprus

I'd like to meet my granddad
But he lives in a land far away,
Where it is hot and sunny.
I hear he is an old man now,
His face is wrinkled like a lemon in the sun.
When we meet
We will talk in Greek
Someday.

While Shohid's dad worked, just down the road from Daneford School, in a Spitalfields garment factory.

My Dad

My dad works in a factory
In a street near Brick Lane.
He is a presser,
He uses a hot iron to smooth the coats,
My dad is tired at the end of the day,
He rests for a while
He does the shopping
Then later we have our dinner,
And go to bed or watch TV for a while.
We watch the nine o'clock news.
Next day my dad wakes up at five o clock
And does praying.
If he is late he prays in the house,
If he is early he prays in the mosque.
Later he has his breakfast –
Sometimes he has 'nun'.
And then he goes to work.

Four years on from this event, one which Westminster had probably never seen the like before: what? Working class children reading their own poems about their own city in the mother of parliaments – and Kinnock's words of commendation for Young World Books were launched back at him as an attack. The Thatcher government was still in power and 1988 was the year of their viciously backward Education Act with its institutionalising of League Tables, OFSTED, attacks on Local Education Authorities, the National Curriculum and all the apparatus of reactionary education ideology. Lady Olga Maitland, the coordinator of 'School Watch', a right wing Conservative parents' group had been set up to campaign against anti-racist and internationalist books that teachers were using in school, particularly London schools, were targeting two publishing initiatives in particular. One was the Institute of Race Relations whose two books *Roots of Racism* and *Patterns of Racism* had been condemned by the Department of Education and Science and their cohorts amongst 'School Watch', who now pounced upon the cartoon book illustrated by the brilliant British artist Christine Smith: *How Racism*

Came to Britain. The DES wallahs called the book 'categorical, aggressive and simplistic', adding that it was 'a polemical and crude strip cartoon'. Siva was the first to jump to its defence clarifying the true purpose behind the attack: 'The next generation must be so ideologically orientated towards this Toryism that they will neither entertain or be allowed independent thinking. That is their objective. We are returning to a cultural imperialism which must make the Tory ideology safe for the next generation.'

As for Young World Books, Maitland used them for a direct attack not only on Kinnock, but on Liberation too. The *Daily Mail* quoted her as saying: 'They are an absolute disgrace. They are totally biased and undermine every aspect of authority. It is absolutely staggering that Neil Kinnock should have been so totally lacking in judgment as to give these books his backing'. The London *Evening Standard* reported a DES spokesman as saying 'We are investigating the suitability of these books to be used with children,' under the headline 'anti-police books get Neil's ok', while the *Daily Telegraph* reported that John Bowis, Conservative MP for Battersea mimicked Kinnock's endorsement of Young World Books in Parliament, and added 'That's the sort of book that the Leader of the Opposition thinks is worthwhile to be passing round classes to the ILEA,' calling Liberation a 'Marxist organisation'. For the particular context of this attack was also a part of the Tory intention of securing the imminent abolition of the Labour-controlled ILEA, and Young World Books was also grist to that mill. As for *The Sun* its reporter one John Kay, picked up on the classroom play of 1989, *Who Killed Michael Ferreira?* which had been published in 1986 in *All Our Words* another Young World Book, edited by me. To Murdoch's *Sun*, the fact that a black youth had been killed on the streets of London and the police had ignored his plight meant nothing, as its headline blazed: 'Kinnock backs anti-cop books for kids'.

Kay Beauchamp, 89 years old at the time and still Secretary both of Liberation and Young World Books, put the true motives around the events with her characteristic succinctness. In an open letter she wrote: 'I myself, nor our editor, the poet, writer and teacher Chris Searle, have received a single complaint from parents, teachers or pupils. Those responsible for Young World Books are bound to ask themselves: 'why the attack now?' Is it the desire to find some means or other of criticising Neil Kinnock or the desire to add fuel to the fire they are stoking up in an attempt to destroy the ILEA or, that they find the books popular with young people? Probably all three.' For me, it was also the first time I had been publicly defended by a relatively new MP, Jeremy Corbyn a strong Liberation supporter. The *Daily Telegraph* report noted that 'Mr Jeremy Corbyn, Labour MP for Islington North, accused Mr Bowis of being 'grossly unfair' to the editor, Christopher Searle, who had done a lot to bring Caribbean culture into London Schools'.

By that time too, like millions of others I had become sickened by the flagrant daily racism of *The Sun*. Supported by the Campaign for Press and Broadcasting Freedom who eventually published it as an 86 page book, I wrote *Your Daily Dose: Racism and The* Sun. In 1986 Rupert Murdoch's News International conglomerate shifted production of all its newspapers to a new East London works at Wapping, East London. This new plant used new computer resources that meant journalists could directly input their copy rather than use print works to set the type, causing the potential redundancy of hundreds of print workers across the industry. The failed strike at Wapping despite the mass courage of print workers, and failure to block distribution of the Murdoch newspapers including *The Times, Sunday Times* and *The Sun* was a huge blow to a free press and gave even greater power to the media conglomerates. It meant that their papers could get away with even baser standards of news distortion and *The Sun* seized its opportunity to become an even deeper cesspit of racism and sexism. The necessary daily research I needed to do by reading *The*

Sun almost every day for a year was sickening enough but I had the pages of the *Morning Star,* for which I was also beginning to write regularly, to act as a daily antidote to the Murdoch poison.

***

Back to October 1983, when I was still at Daneford and like my colleagues, also still wrestling with the strange and sometimes harsh contradictions of the school. Since my return from Grenada I had been deeply involved in the solidarity movement and always in direct contact with the 'Revo's' leadership, particularly Prime Minister Maurice Bishop, Minister of Education Jacqueline Creft and Chief Education Officer – a young St Lucian, Didacus Jules. I had gone back twice to Grenada since I had finished working there in August 1982; once to organise a conference with South African Education and Production pioneer, Patrick Van Rensburg and once to support a group of geographers conducting an energy survey in the island. I was a long way away from events within the Revo and had no idea of the boiling up of tension and division within its leadership. When I had worked very closely with them during 1980–82, they seemed very close and were always powerfully conscious of the menace of disunity, something which the Reagan government were forever trying to foment. My book, *Grenada: The Struggle Against Destabilisation* sought to detail the methods that the U.S Government were using to bring down the Revo, in particular through the CIA and its press arm, USICA. By terrible irony, the very week that the book was due to be published and launched in London, the Revo imploded through its own divisions. The resulting executions of Maurice, Jackie and other stalwarts of the process, and the subsequent U.S. invasion hit me like hammer blows, and it was the solidarity and friendship shown to me by my colleagues and students and Daneford, that saved me from personal collapse, a process that I was later to describe in 1989 in my memoir *Grenada Morning*. I believed so deeply in the Revo's processes and gains, and had argued so strongly and persuaded so many in England of its processes and unity that its collapse went through my blood and brain like a lightning strike, and as I internalised and tried to understand the cause of its factions and divisions, it filled me with incomprehensibility and despair. I had never felt that way before, and it felt that the only answer was to somehow move on, both physically and mentally, by getting out of London and rebuilding my life and consciousness somewhere else where I could make a new start. The shock didn't essentially change my politics – if anything I felt more and more dedicated to a socialist view of the world. But I just felt that somehow I needed to break away, to get out of London, to go somewhere else.

***

By early 1984 the Miners' strike was almost at its zenith, and our National Union of Teachers branch at school had forged a partnership with the National Union of Mineworkers' branch at Shirebrook Colliery in North Derbyshire. Miners from Shirebrook became regular visitors to the school. They would talk to our classes and tell them about miners' lives, so different to that of our students, whether they were white from Hoxton or Bangladeshi from Brick Lane. Their classroom talks and the fascination our boys had with their Derbyshire speech somehow created a rare unity in the classroom. Then at lunchtimes they would talk to us teachers in the staff room, telling us about the progress of the strike, before taking their buckets and 'Coal not Dole' stickers along the market stalls of Bethnal Green Road, where they found a lot of generosity. After they spoke and joked with our students, there were plenty among them who were moved and touched. I remember how Sean, a thirteen-year-old Caribbean boy, immediately got to work on a poem:

The Miner

I must be a living dead man
That's all that's in my head.
My lungs are black as tar.
My life is hanging on a string.
When I cough I feel so dizzy
It's like I would faint.
But when I get out of the mine
My back is arched
And my head is swollen.
And I think I'll die
But I am a miner
And I must survive.

The message of the Shirebrook miners had a deep effect upon teachers and students, and in mid-1984 the NUT members at Daneford were invited by the miners and their families to spend a weekend with them. Twenty or so of us piled into two mini-buses, and when we arrived in Shirebrook we received the warmest of welcomes at the Miners' Welfare Club. I particularly remember how the miners' wives greeted the two Bangladeshi women teaching assistants who came with us. When the wives saw them climb from the mini-buses they made a beeline for them, hugging them and sweeping them off their feet with love as they almost carried them into their homes. It was an unforgettable weekend for us as we learned, exchanged life stories and formed friendships between north and south. Suddenly North Derbyshire and East London was in truth what it was: the same country, the same people.

That weekend also sealed it for me: I needed to find a job up north. I began to apply for anything that I saw, particularly in and around Sheffield. Although I was now over forty and still a low-level scale one teacher, I had lots of experience behind me, both internationally and in inner city London, but carried a lot of left baggage so it was going to be a progressive employer that would have me. I applied for many school and youth work posts in Sheffield and Bradford, but didn't get very far.

Then I found that I had been shortlisted and was invited to two interviews for posts in the advisory service of Sheffield Education Department. The first was Advisory Teacher of Peace Studies – which went to the colleague who was acting in the role – and the second was adviser for Multicultural Education. They were both new posts. When I turned up for interview for the latter, at the time I had no idea about its scope or seniority. I was also deeply suspicious about 'Multicultural Education', having seen how such posts, rather than truly combating racism in the system, were largely ornamental, addressing only the superficialities of racist structures in schools and society. So I wasn't optimistic either about my chances or the nature of the post. What I didn't fully realise was that advisers held the same seniority as headteachers, were responsible for whole-school inspections in the Local Education Authority's schools, had significant curriculum development power and could create new posts and funding for curriculum innovations. When I arrived for the interview at the Education Department I found that the other interviewees were either senior multi-culturalists from other large urban LEAs or head teachers or deputy head teachers. So I was anything but optimistic about my chances.

The only person that I knew in Sheffield was Maurice Jones, the Editor of the National Union of Mineworkers' weekly journal, *The Miner*. I had met him on a visit he had made to Grenada, and we had talked in detail about the progress of the 'Revo'. He invited me to stay with him at his house in Pitsmoor – which ironically was to become the catchment area of the school where I was to become head teacher six years later. Both nights that I stayed with him he had late-evening visits from Arthur Scargill, the President of the NUM and strike leader, to discuss strike strategy and reportage, so suddenly and accidentally I found myself in a strange epicentre. On the evening before the interview I was contacted by Sue Atkins, a youth worker at the African-Caribbean Hub centre in Sharrow, taken there to a meeting with some of its workers, and I also met and talked with her Barbadian husband the remarkable Mike Atkins, a Caribbean activist and keen cricketer who, as a boy from near Oistins, had bowled at the great Barbadian batsmen Everton Weekes and Clyde Walcott in the nets in Queens Park. He told me that his hands were still stinging from the powerful drives that Weekes and Walcott hit back at him every Friday afternoon when he and his friends left school early to go down to the nets to bowl at their heroes.

Mike had worked in the steel industry, had become a careers officer and was now the Director of Sheffield City Council's Race Equality Unit. Clearly a Caribbean radical, he was particularly interested in my time in Grenada. The next day I found that he was on the interviewing panel along with councillors, senior Education Officers and the Chief Adviser. Anyway, whatever I said, however I said it, I was given the job, and as I sat on the train going back to St Pancras nobody was more surprised than me. I had jumped in those few minutes from the most lowly position of the teaching profession to a post equivalent to one of the highest scales. I thought I couldn't make it up!

But it was back to my classes in Bethnal Green for the rest of the school year. I found myself in some trouble again. I had made a speech at the Institute of Education which had been reprinted in the teachers' journal, *Teaching London Kids*. It openly criticized the relativism of 'multicultural education', and added this:

> When we come to consider multicultural education we know it is all things to all people. Anti-racist education is now much defended by teachers throughout the country, but it has taken a long struggle to reach the point where the ILEA is making it a compulsory policy for all their schools. They will have to formulate their policy within the participatory and democratic energy of London's teachers and they will have to live up to it and resource it seriously. But the third stage, anti-imperialist education, is something which challenges everything in our society and in the wider world which is oppressive.

For as soon as we begin to teach about conditions and struggles in such countries as El Salvador, we are beginning to help our children understand the role of imperialism in the world; the role of multinational interests, international financial and economic intrigue and an oppression which exploits, works through yet is beyond racism – which is only one of its strategies. And as we enter into that kind of struggle with knowledge and consciousness, we are undisputedly talking about the source of imperialism in the world, the United States of America.

When the speech was published, it took no time for the *Daily Express* to seize upon it with its Islamophobic headline: 'Beware these classroom Ayatollahs!' Something I'd certainly never been accused of before – I suppose it made a change from 'pied piper', or 'indoctrinator' or 'Mr Squeers'. The Conservative member for Gainsborough and Horncastle and the co-founder of The Coalition for Peace through Security, Edward Leigh MP (he's still there, even now in 2022) kindly quoted from my Institute of Education speech in Parliament, adding that 'Mr Searle's prescription for an anti-racist imperialist syllabus lent weight for 'an anti-indoctrination clause in the Education Act'. Another fervently right wing campaigner, Baroness Cox wrote an article for the *Daily Mail* headlined 'Militants who are getting your children' next to a cartoon of a group of school children in a playground shaped as a hammer and sickle.

These interventions, plus more in the *Times Educational Supplement*, prompted the ILEA to issue me a 'warning' which was widely reported. The *Daily Telegraph* titled their article 'Balanced view warning to anti-US teacher'. The story was also picked up by the *Rand Daily Mail* in Apartheid South Africa, where I was also characterized as 'Anti-US teacher.' As for my disciplining from the ILEA, it was issued by a rather genial but nonplussed Acting Headteacher (the real one was absent with stress at the time), who with something of a bemused smile handed me a copy of the ILEA curriculum document called *History and Social Sciences at the Secondary School Level*, open at the section titled 'teaching controversial issues in the classroom'. I thanked him, read the appointed page and returned to my classroom to carry on teaching a section of the compelling book by the novelist of El Salvador Manlio Argueta, *One Day of Life,* telling with a simple and moving eloquence the experiences and struggles of the ordinary people of El Salvador against a brutal military dictatorship enjoying the compete support of Reagan's US government. For me it was a strange and absurd reprimand, and as I looked around at my students, knowing that many of them too had arrived in that very classroom because of invasion and military suppression in their own birth country now called Bangladesh, made no sense, in either curriculum or human terms, and it made me ask again the same old question that I had asked from my classrooms in Canada, the Caribbean, Mozambique or Stepney a thousand times before: 'What is a school for, if not for life and truth?'

***

Through a relationship of letters I had got to know an educational journalist called Eva Bruck in the German Democratic Republic. She was in her fifties, had been a Jewish refugee in Britain as a child during the war and had returned to East Germany just after the war. She was a critical supporter of her government and had a strong international outlook, which resulted in her spending time in schools in Mongolia, and writing a succession of articles on her experiences for the GDR journal *Teachers of the World.* She had also written about my work and invited me to write for the same journal. I wrote some articles for which there was a small payment in local currency, and she asked me to visit the GDR in order to visit schools and spend the money, as it couldn't be changed in Britain. I spent a fascinating two weeks with her, both in Berlin and Dresden. Like thousands of other GDR citizens she was denoted as a 'victim of fascism' and could travel free with a friend on all trains and buses in the country. She took me to see the massive rebuilding projects in Dresden, which had been so devastated by British bombs and fire storms during the last months of the war, and we spent some deeply communal and enjoyable days at a youth holiday camp.

But one particular visit has never left me: the excursion to Ravensbruck, the death camp for women only, during the Nazi Holocaust. Eva telephoned her friend Rita, a woman in her sixties, and we went as a threesome. Rita had been an inmate at Ravensbruck and knew every square yard of the large preserved site. I couldn't get over the amalgam of horror and beauty around me; for the camp was constructed next to a serene, calm lake which at its upper end had a village with a soaring church spire. Yet at the lake's other extremity was this construction of barbarism and hatred which only three and a half decades earlier had murdered thousands of women: Jews, Roma, Communists and anti-fascists. We had walked all around the camp and now approached the crematorium. On its steps were a couple of young soldiers flirting with a group of young women. Rita saw red. She marched up to the group, berating them for their disrespect to the dead, and rolling up her sleeve and brandishing at them the number that was burnt into her flesh: 75443. The memory of her rage controlled yet full of fire and anger has never left me. As for the group of youths it was as if lightning had struck them, as the young soldiers stood to an embarrassed attention and the girls wandered ashamedly and desultorily away. I stood there, immobilized, ever thankful.

As we parted, Rita gave me a book, a narrative of Ravensbruck victims and heroes, with the inscription above her number: 'for peace and friendship'. Never had these two words meant so much. I wrote a poem to her which was published in my collection *Red Earth*. Its last six lines were, simply:

Woman!
Maker and continuer
Teller of life!

Your story is the chorus
Of our century,
Our history.

As I finished at Daneford I had one last task to do for Young World Books. I had been sent some stories, poems and a play by Grenadian writers, and wanted to make sure that they were published in a memorial volume. Dan Jones drew a series of evocative illustrations and the book, *Callaloo* came out in 1984 shortly before I left for Sheffield. The book's title referred to a popular soup based on leaves from the dasheen plant, and was also the title of poet Merle Collins' rampaging poem about human unity – 'All o'we/in allo' dis world/so mix up/like callaloo' – a lesson so ironically and tragically learned from the implosion of the 'Revo'. Merle who later became famed and celebrated, as a poet and a novelist, both in Britain and America would read this poem to thousands at open air rallies across the nation.

Another contributor was Jacob Ross, ex-cultural officer in Grenada's Ministry of Education whose stories opened *Callaloo*, and he too became recognized over the years as a major Caribbean writer. As I put together the book in 1984 I could only reflect on what had been gained and what had been lost and Maurice's final words to me: 'It ent easy, man', words I was to discover the truth of many more times in Sheffield. For leaving London for Sheffield was to become another migration for me. I felt I had to go. Certainly Grenada's tragedy had impelled me.

I had written what I thought at the time was one last book, a study of the extraordinary ways that the process of the "Revo" had impacted on language – formally, informally, as a tool of struggle and learning, a connection with the world – but most crucially as an assertion of revolutionary selfhood, comradeship, humour and love. The book was like a riposte to myself and what I had written after teaching in Tobago, *The Forsaken Lover*. I was writing about how language changes fundamentally when ordinary people take power in their lives at all levels: the political, the personal, the cultural, the pedagogical. How language fuses standard forms, Creole forms, national and international forms in a nexus of revolutionary change in all they say, sing, write and do. *Words Unchanged: Language and Revolution in Grenada* I called it, dedicating it to Maurice Bishop and Jacqueline Creft. I thought then, as I think now, it was the most useful book I had ever written. As Ngugi wrote in his introduction: '*Words Unchained* is a dream unchained, the dream of an awakened people, and no power on earth can stop the march forward of such a people. They will struggle to unchain their hands, their minds, their collective soul. How do you kill a dream remembered?' It also became a stimulus for my life and work in Sheffield.

Chapter 3
Stranger in a Steel City

I used to pass over the Don Valley on my way to University in Leeds in the early Sixties; I saw the huge smoking mass of the steelworks in Attercliffe and Brightside, the flames of their retorts and the pall of smoggy polluted air that enveloped them. It never occurred to me that I would ever be working in that mighty steel city – the fourth largest conurbation in England with its excess of 700,000 people. I'd been a stranger in a steel city before when I'd emigrated to Canada's steel city Hamilton on Lake Ontario with its huge steel works. Yet now this was my own country, in the same county where I had spent my Leeds University years. Here I was in the middle of Sheffield in Leopold Street, ensconced in its education offices almost opposite the Victorian municipal palace of its Town Hall with the statue of Mercury atop of its tower and its main chamber the Mandela Room, stretching the length of its first storey. But it was the downtown block of St James where I found the most inspiration. Its top floor was the temporary HQ of the National Union of Mineworkers, and it was their struggle that had truly brought me to Sheffield. One of my first tasks when I came to the City was to interview for *Race & Class*, the miner-poet Bill Ross, whose strike anthology *Against All the Odds* was hugely popular and inspiring all around the South Yorkshire pit communities

Sheffield Education Department seemed more like a university complex than a centre of local schools administration. There were a host of education and staffing officers and more than twenty advisers most of them having advisory teachers working with them. The Chief Adviser had an academic background and most of the education officers saw the advisers as sitting in plum posts, over-promoted and overpaid. A group of them would drive off to pubs on the outskirts of the city on most lunchtimes, sinking a few pints and criticising conditions in the schools they 'advised'. One said to me soon after I'd arrived 'You're all right here Chris, just take it easy and you've got a job for life.' And he smiled, clutched his car keys and drove off to the pub. Other advisers worked hard and conscientiously, proud to be a part of a local education authority which was solidly and proudly comprehensive and non-school uniform, gave substantial extra positive action funding to struggling schools in depressed neighbourhoods, and in many curriculum areas like Music, Languages, Youth Work, Peace Studies and Agricultural Studies was making unique and exemplary advances.

The Chief Education Officer, newly appointed, was Bill Walton. He was ex-RAF, so I remembered feeling a little

Bill Walton: Sheffield's Chief Education Officer: 1985-90'

nervous that he wouldn't be very supportive of my curriculum areas, but I needn't have been because he was deeply committed and openly supported local black communities with policies and resources, and was always well disposed towards me and my strategies. He also insisted that Mike Atkins be at the centre of all anti-racist initiatives of the Education Department, something that pleased me enormously. He strongly admired Mike and the way he had set about removing racist barriers in other Council departments and now it was time for the same to be done in his own. He set in motion weekly meetings with Mike who came over from the town hall, myself and other officers and made it clear to all that the LEA needed to make rapid progress on the anti-racist front. Sheffield during the mid-eighties did not have a large black community. Pakistani, Yemeni, and Bengali workers had worked in the steel industry from the Sixties onwards in the low paid and frequently most dangerous jobs, but since the early 1980's economic crisis in the steelworks, particularly in Attercliffe and Darnall in the north of the city, there was serious unemployment and hardship. There was also minimal English as a Second language resources within schools, just three Community Languages teachers and few resources to support the African–Caribbean children in schools despite the exemplary role played by Sheffield Youth Service, mainly serving school leavers. Dramatist Mustapha Matura said that it was visiting a Sheffield youth club in the early seventies that had given him the inspiration to write his classic *Welcome Home Jacko*, which had moved my own East London students so much a few years before.

It did not take me long to decide what my priorities would be. I needed to help create structures within schools which would enable teachers to find the confidence and skills to tackle racism in their midst. There was also an obvious need to recruit and promote many more black colleagues in schools. Sheffield had no black headteachers or black colleagues in senior management positions. The LEA needed to devise a strategy to create many more resources for black school students and those in further education. And the school and colleges' curriculum needed to be radically transformed so that all school populations – students, teachers and parents – could begin to conceive of Sheffield as a major multiracial city with communities of powerful histories and cultures. I felt anything but alone in tackling these tasks. Very soon I got to know, talk with and seek advice from activists in all communities and arranged regular meetings with their community organisations including the Yemeni Community Association, the Pakistani Muslim Centre, the Bengali Community Association and Sheffield and District African Caribbean Association (SADACCA) at their large centre on The Wicker in the city centre.

I had no car, being one of life's pedestrians, and soon became a regular traveller on Sheffield's marvellous and marvellously cheap bus service. I could go anywhere, to schools all over a very hilly city with one of the largest land areas in Britain. I got to know many of the drivers too who were invariably friendly and full of quips, particularly when they recognised from my voice that I was a Londoner. 'Reet 'ere love!' one would shout out at me as I reached the closest point to the school that I'd asked for, or 'Next stop duck!' Through them I soon got to know all the byways of Sheffield, whether I was going to Handsworth to see a headteacher about a sheaf of racist jokes that a black parent had found in the school playground – what was he going to do about that? 'What's the problem? They're only jokes', he told me. Or the short ride to Pye Bank and the old Victorian school looking down over the centre of the city. The first time I was at the Nursery First School there, I taught the children, many of whom were from Caribbean families – a fisherman's song I had learned from my students in Tobago, *Aza Buil' One New Boat*. The next time I went there the headteacher presented me with a beautiful picture book of drawings and paintings by the children illustrating every verse. And in Kettlebridge Primary children sang a song in assembly in Bengali. I began to feel a very lucky man and I found myself loving Sheffield and its huge cultural potential.

But it wasn't all congenial when I began to take up the issue of school exclusions, particularly what seemed to be the large number of exclusions of black children. At Springfield Primary School, close to the city centre in Broomhall a whole clutch of ten year old children, black and white, had been excluded for largely petty reasons. I told the headteacher that this was unacceptable. She angrily complained about me to senior education officers, one of whom told me that I shouldn't argue with headteachers. What was I there for then? I rejoined. Were our schools going to be exclusive or inclusive? In Abbeydale Grange Secondary School, black parents were complaining about the disproportionate number of black exclusions. When I discussed the issue with Mike, we concluded that we needed an exclusions survey to establish the facts. The results of the survey told us that the parents were right; they showed that in secondary schools where most of the black students attended, black exclusions prevailed at a strongly distorted level.

As I got to know schools the length and breadth of Sheffield I began to realise that I was working in a powerfully multilingual city despite there being a black population of eleven or twelve thousand, a much smaller black population than in other large Yorkshire cities like Leeds or Bradford. On one of my visits to Pye Bank school I went with the Guyana-born poet and children's writer John Agard. He loved the school and its children, reading poems to them in his deep Caribbean Creole vernacular. The children, white, Caribbean, Pakistani, Somali and Yemeni, loved them. As he walked in the playground with them, he noticed and laughed about the pigeon droppings on the slate roof and stone walls of the old buildings. He set down an instant poem, which he read to them with huge West Indian mirth, wit, rhyme and gesticulation.

Pigeon Eye View

I'm a little pigeon
    And I do
      More than coo
On your school wall
I leave a mark or two
Some call it dropping
I call it pigeon topping

Some also call it poo
But to me
And my artistic pigeon family
It is simply
      Pigeon graffiti

John Agard in 1984.

He had touched something deep and precious in their brains and hearts, in their own language.

When I met and talked with the itinerant Bengali teacher Mahmood who, playing his harmonium like Bishri and Abdus Salique had done in Spitalfields and the Half Moon Theatre, I began to understand why his language and that of the Bengali children at Kettlebridge that he taught was so crucial to them all, here too in the heart of Sheffield. Mahmood told me how much his mother tongue meant to him and all Bangladeshis now living in England. 'Bengali is a highly developed language that has been the vehicle of a great tradition of novels and poetry,' he told me. 'I'm not just talking about Nobel prize winner Tagore, but all the thousands of our writers and a whole world of literature which passes unnoticed by thousands of Bengalis living in England. We need to introduce them to a culture from which they have often moved away. As a proud Bengali I want to bring this culture back to all the people of Britain – our music, our song, our poetry. Not only by translation which can only ever bring a limited appreciation, but through trying to introduce the beauty of

Mahmood Rahman in 1984.

the language itself – the images, rhythms and sounds –
through our songs. This song for example is a song of
freedom of revolution, which arose from the Indian
people's cultural movement during the struggle for a united
India.' And he sang to me in Bengali words which he later
translated:

The language of my protest
The fire of my resistance
Burns and burns again
In the huge meaning of my revolt
It grinds and destroys all conspirators
Bringing purpose and light
To the hearts of thousands

He told me about the events of 21st February 1952, a day
of protest in Dacca, East Pakistan as it was then, to give
Bengali an equal status with Urdu, the official language
of West Pakistan, as a national language. 'At least ten
people died, but in the confusion it was impossible to know
the exact number. But the repression sparked off a huge

popular rage and more and more protests were held against the ruthless Pakistani regime that was imposing such undemocratic rule upon our people. The day became symbolic for us. It represented our rejection of all forms of injustice and oppression. This was the day we really got to know ourselves. We discovered on this day the right to our own language. This was inseparable for our national struggle. On this day we take all our resolution and determination to be free. We re-emerge every year on this day as a new people, and this is through our will to retain and develop our language and culture.' I had worked closely with Bengali students and parents in their largest British communities in East London, yet I only learned all this in Sheffield.

The embrace of words that I found among Sheffield's Black and arrivant communities went deep into the history and roots of all Sheffielders. Through her poetry and performances as part of the three women comedy act 'The Chuffinelles', I got to know the poet Margaret Barraclough.

Margaret Barraclough at Earl Marshal School, 1990

Born in 1925 she began work in the steel industry at sixteen. She was one of the first women steelworkers to work alongside men in the rolling mills and later worked as a crane driver and operator of fork lift trucks. She began writing poems as a crane driver, leaving messages in verse for the next shift worker in the crane cabs, and this love of verse and rhyme soon developed into a crafting of much longer and deeper Sheffield dialect poems, like her salute to Attercliffe, the steel neighbourhood where she had lived, but was now an amalgam of dereliction, sex shops, abandoned facades and a huge prospective shopping centre Meadowhall, a part of the huge social divide that was Sheffield, with its prosperous 'white highlands' to the south and its much more downpressed and struggling public housing estates and multiracial neighbourhoods to the north: where wealth and poverty coexisted in an uneasy dichotomy.

The Death of a District

Oh Attercliffe, dear Attercliffe, what 'ave they
    done to thee?
It breaks my 'eart to see 'er after what she
    used to be.

From Weshford Bridge to Weedon Street 'er arms
    were open wide;
She sheltered an' protected us from t'rest o'
    t' world ahtside.

She 'ad a gret big thumpin 'eart that everybody felt;
We luvved 'er an' she luvved us back na matter
    we'er we dwelt.

Remember t'Cliffe on a Satdy? Thad meet
    dozens o'people tha knew,
An' stand laughin' an' jokin' until tha remembered
    abaht shoppin' thad promised to do.
If ye din't live down theer then ye'll not understand
    what the warmth o'these people wa worth;
They din't make no fuss, or use fancy words; but tha
    knew, they wer't salt o' the earth.

If ya a'nt got much money ya din't 'ave to fret:
This allas be summat thad manage to get.
Shopkeepers wer' great, an so understandin'; they
    knew thad a struggle to pay;
Sometimes the'd seh 'Tek it owd luv and pay me
next week, I know thall not run away.'

God bless 'em and keep 'em they wer all worth their weight
Wee aht their 'elp, lots o'kids 'ad 'ave now't to eyt.

Remember t'owd Attercliffe Palace, thid tell jokes
    an' thid dance an' thid sing;
An' if that got sat back o' them pillars, thad 'ad it
    tha cudn't see a thing.
Remember an' all, all the fun that we'd 'ave in the
    Regal, the 'Delph', the Globe an' the Pav;
We dint need no nightclubs, an fancy cafes,
Wid cum aht o' t' pictures an' 'ave pie an' pehs.

If tha wanted a pub crawl, an tha cud affoord
Thi were pubs ev'ry few yahds on each side o' t'roord.
On Satday nights, the streets would errupt
Foorks sed it were all that Stones bitter thi supped.
Yed see 'em go aht, lookin' spotless an' neat:
Then cum in black and bleedin' thru feightin in
    t' street.
Dear friend I can see there's a tear in your eye;
Then ya must be from theer like me.
Thiv tern aht that gret thumpin' 'eart that we
    knew, an' whose luv we'ad shared so free.
Na don't get me wrong, we all wanted to move,
The soot an' the grime made life 'ahd.
An' the clouds o' red dust that ed blot out the sun
    an' then settle on t'weshin in t'yard.
We wanted 'ouse wi a gahden an' bath an fresh
    air in us lungs, nothin' moor
('cept for a lavvy in t'ouse, an' 'ot watter int'
    tap an' a few dozen roses round t'door.)
Now that big dirty beast lier theer dyin', but ya
    won't 'ear us givin' three cheers.
'cos we luvved er an we'd like to thank 'er for all those
    wonderful years.
So we'll miss ya, owd luv for the rest of our lives
Wi got our nice 'ouse with ot'watter in t'tap,
But was the price that we paid too high?

It was as if I'd never left them, the bonds between language, race and class. Agard had showed me that again at Pye Bank; Mahmood in Kettlebridge and Margaret in Attercliffe; as my students and their parents had showed me, in Spitalfields, Stepney, the Basement and Poplar, in Tobago, Grenada and Mozambique too. For here in Sheffield, whatever resources we were going to win and develop, it was clear that languages, their plurality and their richness, would be at their centre, in the struggle to create a multilingual city from the heart of its schools.

I was learning much about Sheffield from the teachers and students I met, but nobody taught me more than Bill Moore. He was the proudest of Sheffielders, born in 1911 and brought up by his grandparents in Attercliffe after his mother died from puerperal fever when he was two weeks old and his father two days before his 30th birthday was killed in Ypres in 1917. His grandfather, a retired ex-policeman, kept pigs in the heart of Attercliffe to supplement his pension. Bill was awarded a scholarship to Sheffield's most exclusive school, King Edward VII Grammar, and made his first anti-war protest by refusing point-blank to join the school's officer training corps. In nineteen thirty he was awarded a further scholarship to Oriel College, Oxford to study History, and took part in the student union debate, passing the resolution 'In no circumstances would we fight for king and country'. The death of his father and millions of others, mostly working class men who had been sent to war by the profiteers and warmongers, made him an ardent peace campaigner.

After he left Oxford he threw himself into the Communist Party, the peace and anti-fascist movements, the solidarity movements with Ethiopia, Spain and the rest of the struggling world and during the 1939–45 war he was posted to Nigeria, teaching Nigerian troops and learning about the power of British imperialism on the African earth. After the war he returned to Sheffield as a teacher and helped to organise the 1950 World Peace Conference in the city, a conference that never happened. The British Labour government refused to give visas to its delegates, including Paul Robeson, the Chilean poet Pablo Neruda and the Soviet composer Shostakovich. The party secretary had declared that taking part in the Congress would be incompatible with membership. Bill told me that walking along the street opposite the Town Hall at the time, he accidentally bumped into a passer-by. Bill was really tall, and the unknown passer-by was short. As Bill looked down, he saw it was Pablo Picasso looking up at him. He remembered sitting at the next table to the great artist in a café opposite the Town Hall, as he drew doves on serviettes and napkins which he handed out to the delegates to the conference that never was. The refusal to admit the great Neruda was a signal irony considering the welcome many Chilean refugees found in Sheffield after the fascist coup in Chile in September 1973. A new community was born in the city. Bill would tenaciously tell me about Sheffield's history of progress and internationalist reform: how at the time of the French Revolution the British government were more frightened about a similar upsurge happening in Sheffield than any other city in England; about the militant petition to the King in the 1790s to end slavery in the British empire; about the door to door campaign in the 1820s to ban West Indian sugar because of the brutality of the plantation owners; the petition to ban compensation to slave owners after slavery formally ended in 1833; the campaigning to support the slave-opposing forces in the American civil war; the call of the Sheffield Trades Council to stop the war against the Irish in 1921 and in 1927 to stop the war against China. Bill had it all and much more imprinted on his historical memory, and no events more telling than those around the betrayal of the physical force Chartist Samuel Holberry whose insurrection was put down in 1840, its leaders imprisoned, with Holberry dying in York prison in 1842, aged twenty-seven. Bill loved Holberry's memory and tradition – his grandmother had known Mary Holberry, Sam's activist widow. He established the

Bill Moore standing beside the Holberry Cascades
Peace Gardens in Sheffield 1998.

Holberry Society to keep alive his memory. When the
Sheffield Peace Gardens were reconfigured in 1998, the
fountains were called the 'Holberry Cascades', provoked by
Bill's militant campaigning. As was a plaque commemorat-
ing the struggle and sacrifice of those South Yorkshire men
who were members of the International Brigades in Spain
during the Civil War. Bill wrote passionately of Sheffield's
brave working class history in the last two sentences of his
autobiographical account *History from Below* published in
2005: 'I know of no city anywhere in the world whose citizens have a finer history of unremitting struggle, yet our
children are taught none of it. So here's to the day when
they will all know!' Bill taught me so much and I will never
forget his words. My task, as with all teachers, was to carry
this on and fulfil his dream of knowledge and action for all

our children, and I made my first efforts by writing a young people's play about Samuel and Mary Holberry and the Chartist struggle in Sheffield. It's called *Holberrys*, and I dedicated it to Bill.

Meanwhile, I was traversing the city's schools, holding meetings with teachers and trying to urge them to set up anti-racist committees. Some headteachers were not pleased at this strategy, suspecting that it might create an alternative locus of power in their schools to theirs, but I found myself helped when Bill Walton established a unique approach of 'School-focused Secondments' right across Sheffield's Secondary Schools, whereby Sheffield used the Department for Education's national secondment system for the purpose of benefiting and democratising schools, by seconding two elected colleagues from each school so that they were freed up from teaching duties for the purpose of generating ideas and strategies of teachers to improve school structures, methodology and community involvement within their schools. It was a profoundly progressive measure intended to raise teacher confidence, participation and activism and as such was strongly supported by teachers' unions and parents groups. It also gave teachers more mobilising power to organise teacher-led initiatives like anti-racist committees.

But there were also the key issues of more resources for Black students and much greater recruitment and promotion opportunities for Black colleagues. How would we achieve this? I would sit down with Mike and we would try to come up with a strategy that could be effective in schools, vitally connected to Black communities and without creating huge Council and LEA expenditure. Mike had established many posts across Council departments, which used money granted by the Home Office under Section Eleven of the Local Government Act. This meant that if a local council could provide 25% of the cost of a post specifically and provenly servicing Commonwealth Immigrant communities, the Home Office would pay the balance of 75%, so in brief a local council could get four posts for the

price of one. Of course it depended firstly on an LEA administration prepared to give over mainstream posts to support
the scheme, and secondly on each new post being carefully
scrutinized by Her Majesty's Inspectors (HMI), to verify
that it properly served the families of 'Commonwealth
Immigrants'. It was soon revealed that Sheffield Education
Department did not have a good record on the funding.
When Mike and I examined current Section Eleven provi-
sion in Sheffield Schools, it was clear there was some abuse
and we needed to own up to it if we were to gain Home
Office trust. This wasn't going to be easy. It was the era of
the right wing Thatcher government intent on crushing
socialist and perceived 'loony left' local education authorities like the ILEA and Sheffield, so I wasn't hopeful. But
being entirely honest and declaring and admitting to some
misuse of funds – for example we discovered that a Deputy
Headteacher in one school with a proportion of Black children was being wrongfully paid through Section Eleven,
and in another it was a Head of Religious Education –
seemed to gain Sheffield some respect in the Home Office
and within the HMI, particularly when these wrongful
posts were promptly returned to mainstream funding.
Mike Atkins' influence was signal; he was powerfully
esteemed in the Home Office even up to the level of the
Minister himself.

So, with Bill Walton's commitment that he would
sanction the use of mainstream posts for Section Eleven
conversion, Mike and I began to plan a structure that we
would call Sheffield Unified Multicultural Education
Service (SUMES) that eventually grew to 160-plus Section
Eleven-funded posts. It became one of the largest 'multicultural' cohorts in Britain, and the envy of many other urban
LEAs

The structure we devised, with Mike's ideas at its centre,
was relatively simple: there would be a number of related
sections of teachers, each led by a co-ordinator who would
be at the seniority level of a primary headteacher. The
largest section would be of teachers of English as a Second

SUMES 1986: A new workforce.

Language, to radically increase and unify school-based resources. There was an African–Caribbean Curriculum and Pastoral Development Service, to address issues of language, curriculum and particularly school exclusions across the city. Also a team of Community Liaison teachers to embolden and develop school links with black communities. We also planned a Special Needs team – including a Section Eleven funded educational psychologist, and a Translation and Interpretation Service. The SUMES colleagues would be led by a Director who would be an education officer, and we would create a centre with space for cultural events, meetings, classes, administration needs and a Library and resource centre on the top floor of Springfield School where all teachers in Sheffield schools would be welcomed, particularly the resource centre which would eventually be named in honour of Mike.

With a powerful historical irony, the late nineteenth century pile of Springfield School had been built, like thousands of urban schools throughout Britain following the passage of W.E. Forster's Education Act of 1870. On its exterior sandstone walls was a perfectly preserved bas-relief celebrating the school's original construction. Under an arch of Yorkshire roses are the Words 'Sheffield School Board 1875' and between them the colonialist heraldry of the head of a warrior woman encircled by a military belt carrying the inscription 'Dei Gratia Sciencia Proderit'. The belt is pierced by eight fearsome arrows with large steel heads, surrounded by an anvil, the head of a prominent tusked elephant, a stone fort, two crossed scimitars, and a cannon. Now, with the advent of SUMES, behind these stark images memorialising the apex of empire and militarism was a centre of internationalist, multilingual and anti-racist knowledge in the heart of a great British ex-imperial industrial city which had produced its steel to be sent all over the colonised world. SUMES would help to turn Sheffield's imperial history around.

It was a large-scale project certainly, which would have the capacity to radically change the opportunities for black young people throughout Sheffield schools, and increase the numbers of black and bilingual colleagues across the city. It also increased the number of community language teachers of Urdu and Bengali, plus the first Arabic teacher, who would give particular opportunities to Yemeni students in particular to study their first language up to GCSE level. Early childhood education was not neglected; an under fives service was a part of the SUMES structure with sixteen nursery assistants to be appointed, under a pre-school co-ordinator, and four new posts of Education Welfare officers were to be appointed to attend in particularly to black pupils not attending, or having difficulty attending regularly primary and secondary schools.

The proposal was approved by the Home Office, and we began to begin making appointments in early 1986. The Director of SUMES became Ahmed Gurnah, a Zanzibari of Yemeni roots, who was recruited from Sheffield Polytechnic, where he had been a Lecturer of Sociology. As we embarked upon and carried though the recruitment, we appointed colleagues from all over the country, and very quickly there was a rapid increase in the numbers of black and bilingual colleagues across the LEA, all of whom were given permanent contracts. We set up a part-time teacher education course in collaboration with Sheffield Polytechnic, later Sheffield Hallam University, through which new unqualified recruits to SUMES, on full pay, would study to achieve qualified teacher status within three years.

Over six months the Sheffield teaching force became considerably diversified and culturally and linguistically substantially changed, thanks to SUMES, Bill Walton and particularly Mike Atkins whose consistent pressure had broken through decades of inaction and prejudice. A real test would be how many of these SUMES teachers would go on in the LEA becoming mainstream funded colleagues? Over the years many have, with some achieving senior management posts at primary and secondary levels. So much so that a colleague with Kenyan Asian background and ex-head of the ESL service became one of the city's most brilliant primary school head teachers, and like the present head teacher of King Edward VII School, Bill Moore's old school and the most celebrated and academically successful and still comprehensive, is a woman who first came to Sheffield as a young SUMES colleague working for the African-Caribbean Support Service.

But despite SUMES, the struggle to achieve true appreciation and just respect and promotion within mainstream schools for Black teachers remained a formidable one.

This was illustrated vividly in Tinsley, on the north-eastern edge of the city south of the Don Valley and other side of the M1, where for generations steel workers' families had lived. By the 1980s it had become a popular neighbourhood for Pakistanis and its three schools were experiencing substantial 'white flight' with many white parents sending their children further afield to Brinsworth, which was a part of Rotherham and controlled by Rotherham LEA. It was a testing situation and the rolls of the Tinsley Schools were falling, so much so that Park House Secondary was veering towards closure. In the midst of these circumstances the headship of Tinsley Junior School became vacant. Some of the Primary advisers and councillors involved in the appointments procedure saw the opportunity, as they thought it, of restoring local confidence in the school by appointing a strong white headteacher, but the obvious candidate was the widely experienced Shafique Khan, who was a serving teacher at the school. He'd been a headteacher in Pakistan, was fluent in Urdu and Panjabi as well as English and was well respected by parents. Ahmed was

Shafique Khan

87

also on the interviewing panel, and as a very canny and persuasive member, managed to secure his appointment, but the process again showed what black colleagues were up against in the process of promotion. When the headship of Tinsley Nursery First school came up a few months later there was similar contention and arguments but again the struggle was won as Bertilee Henry, a mature, talented and warmly popular Caribbean colleague in the SUMES under-five service also won the day.

Ahmed had responded to the need for increased literacy within Sheffield's Black communities by devising a community literacy campaign. It was multilingual in character by involving young literacy assistants from the Pakistani, Yemeni and Bengali communities, and had a deep community orientation. Its classes were held in community venues, and it emboldened many young community activists and gave them a new motivation towards their own educational futures, as well as those whom they taught. It showed that SUMES was determined to be within the heartsblood of the community, as well as at the pulse of the schools. As for me, I began a campaign of support and campaigning for the Ethiopian Literacy campaign. The famine and extreme hunger suffered by the Ethiopian people in the mid-eighties created a deep compassion among British people, but one of the downsides of all the charitable work was that the people of Ethiopia were often characterised as helpless, incapable of solving their own problems in deeply negative terms. The schools-based 'Literacy in Ethiopia' campaign was a movement in support of a remarkable achievement of the people – a multilingual literacy campaign (in seventeen languages) which showed Ethiopians in an entirely positive and creative light, educating each other in villages, urban centres and remote locations throughout the huge nation. Sheffield schools, parents, teachers and children organised sponsored walks, swims, bring-and-buy sales, discos, raffles, concerts to raise money for 'A Million Pencils for Ethiopia' – which became the city-wide slogan.

'A million pencils for Ethiopia.'

After we raised the first thousand pounds and I made contact with the Ethiopian Embassy, I was invited to Ethiopia to observe and write about the Literacy Campaign. For me it was an extraordinary experience. I spent time both in working class neighbourhoods of Addis Ababa and in villages in Sidamu province, close to the southern border with Kenya and saw the astonishing creativity of those who at the most local levels, organised and resourced the campaign. It was wonderful to be back in Africa again, and I met and interviewed many educators at all levels. When I returned I wrote a short book which I called *A Blindfold Removed*, which was a powerful metaphor used to describe the effect of the campaign on millions of Ethiopians and the opening up of their futures.

While in Addis, I visited the grave of one of my heroes, Sylvia Pankhurst, militant suffragette, avowed socialist of East London and ceaseless campaigner for the Ethiopian people during the Thirties era of invasion of their nation by Mussolini's fascist Italian forces. When I returned, I wrote this poem to her:

To Sylvia, under the Eucalyptus Trees

I had to look hard to find you
In the holes of sunlight
There under the eucalyptus leaves
Among the stones of Ethiopian patriots

I asked the man who kept the cathedral
Where were you lying?
And in our foreign words of Europe
I stumbled out your name
That I had known in the streets of Bow
In the dreadnought of our people's struggle

Loving what you had done
In the life of two continents,
I read a poem of children over your bones
And saw the flesh of the future all around us
As I watched them playing in their pathways
That lead from Africa
To the blocks of London

1989 was the tenth anniversary of the death of Blair Peach, and we arranged a tribute meeting at the SUMES centre in Springfield School with speakers Suresh Grover from The Southall Monitoring Group and Blair's partner Celia Stubbs. I was also working on a tribute anthology *One for Blair*, to be published by Young World Books with vivid illustrations by Christine Smith, the artist of the Institute of Race Relations' comic book, *How Racism Came to Britain*, which had given so much pique to Lady Olga Maitland and her friends. The anthology was to be launched at the Dominion Centre in Southall in April, with an array of poets, politicians and campaigners from Tariq Ali, Paul Boateng MP and John La Rose, to writers like Joan Riley, Mahmood Jamal, Elean Thomas and David Edgar. Sally Flood from the Basement Writers of nearly twenty years before was also there. There were so many speakers and poets that the rally went on almost until midnight, full of Blair's rebellious and joyous spirit.

As for *One For Blair* it was well received, a combination of new poems and classic poems from all over the world, from Brecht to Ho Chi Minh and Mahmoud Darwish of Palestine, to Daisy Zamora of Nicaragua to Turkey's Nazim Hikmet, Pakistan's Faiz Ahmad Faiz, Jamaica's Elean Thomas and Guyana's Grace Nichols. It was of a world that Blair taught for and struggled for, and I only wished that he could have read all those poems and heard all those poets at the Dominion Centre. As it was we were still left with his murderers free, untried and unpunished, as Michael Rosen and Suzannah Steel told us in their poem, a reworking of *Edward, Edward,* one of the oldest of English ballads:

Who Killed Blair Peach?

what's that on your hands, son?
what's that on your hands?
    only a spot of blood, mum
    only a spot of blood
how did it get there, son?
how did it get there, then?
    must have been a nose-bleed, mum
    must have been me nose
what's this down your coat son
what's this down your coat?
    looks like blood an'all mum
    looks like blood an'all
that was never your nose, son

that was never your nose
    must have come from one of the others
    must have come from from one of our men
but its all in your boots and socks, son
its all in your boots and socks
    in all the course of duty, mum
    all in the course of me job
these stains will never come out, son
these stains will never come out
    they'll be put in the bin and forgot, mum
    they'll be put in the bin and forgot
they'll fix you up with new ones, son
they'll fix you up like new
but I'll remember this, son, I'll remember this
you came home with blood on your boots
from a day of keeping the peace.

The books still kept coming, in Sheffield too. Together with the Sheffield Council for Racial Equality's Principal Race Relations Officer and a powerful poet herself, Debjani Chatterjee, I helped compile *Peaces,* a collection of poems for peace. The dove on its cover reminded me of Bill Moore's 1950 Sheffield encounter with Picasso, as did fourteen-year-old Jonathan Atkinson's *The Dove of Peace*, with its simple rhyming wisdom and profundity.

The dove of peace is flying high,
Watching all the world go by
People are good, people are bad
People are happy, people are sad.
The world is very bad at times,
With all the fighting, all the crimes.
The world is full of grief and sorrow,
Hoping for a new tomorrow.
Racist slogans sprayed on walls,
Equality has no chance at all.
If people could see face to face
It would make the world a better place.
If people could see eye to eye
The dove would descend from the deep blue sky.

Children of Steel, was published by Sheffield Libraries in 1988. It was the closest anthology I'd done to *Stepney*

Words ever since that furore, and the poems concentrated on the huge changes that had happened in the city following the collapse of the steel industry. I invited many schools to send their students' poems about how they saw the future of their city. As Amanda expressed it in her *Fight for Life*, there was a new world ahead and she was confronting it: She began uncompromisingly:

> I am the generation of youth
> I am the generation of truth
> Listen to what I have to say
>
> I am a black person of culture
> I am a black person of pride
> I will not run and hide
>
> Ripped out of history
> Thrown out of time,
> You cannot steal my destiny,
> For it is divinely mine

And Katie's choric couplet and refrain had a similar sense of tenacity and determination:

> This is our city now maybe forever,
> We've got to fight and stay together.

And eleven year old Rupert looked back at other generations, and forward too in his own life:

Sheffield's Future

> My granddad said Sheffield wer' proud
> And its cutlery works wer' well known.
> It made knives and forks by the thousand
> And sent them all over the globe
>
> My dad says Sheffield's gone down
> And it's heading to doom and to fail.
> The fox roams where steelworks once stood
> At Rother Valley you play and sail.

Me and my sister wer' born 'ere
And we want to work 'ere when we're grown.
All Sheffield needs is attention
Some Yorkshire grit and backbone.

But I think Sheffield's grand
New jobs are needed it's true.
We've so much to offer the people,
So who can help Sheffield but you?

The collective intent of the poems was impressive, as if a whole new Steel City generation was speaking. It impressed novelist Barry Hines too. The writer of *A Kestrel for a Knave* wrote as a back cover blurb:

> *Children of Steel* is a collection of poems by Sheffield schoolchildren about their home city. There is an inevitable sense of loss in many of the poems about the destruction of the steel industry and the resultant loss of jobs. But the general tone is not backward-looking or defeatist. There is a feeling of a generation fighting back, determined to make the future work.

***

My access to schools made it easy to pursue chosen curriculum themes. Ethiopian literacy was certainly one of them, but also the struggle against apartheid in South Africa. SUMES helped with an exhibition mounted by teachers on an anti-apartheid theme at Hurlfield School on the Manor, one of Sheffield's most struggling housing estates. Oliver Tambo, the African National Congress President and lawyer colleague of Nelson Mandela came to that and was very appreciative, and with the help of teachers across primary and secondary schools we organised a day's workshop for school students on an anti-apartheid theme in the huge Mandela room in the town hall, ending in a large scale meeting where George Johannes of the ANC (who had visited our school in Poplar, East London) addressed students and Council Leader David Blunkett made a

Freedom Childrem: poems for South African youth.

supportive speech. But one of the most original projects was the poetry anthology *Freedom Children* of 1988, which we subtitled *A tribute in poetry to the young people of South Africa, from the young people of Sheffield*. I had gone to many schools to stimulate the students' writing, and found a keen and willing response. I read poems to them by Oswald Mtshali, Wally Mongane Serote and Dennis Brutus, and the young Sheffielders' response was both moving and perceptive. In all the poetry projects I had been a part of over three decades of teaching, I don't think I had ever encountered such strength of empathy as these Sheffield children's imaginings of the lives and struggles of young people in South African villages and townships. As one fifteen-year-old girl Sallie put it so succinctly in her briefest of poems

Immortal

They'll live forever
And never die
They're joined to us
More than ever

We breathe for them
Fight for them
Live for them
We *are* them.

Or as an anonymous poet of Firth Park School left on his or her desk after a session, a poem they called *Feelings,* it was as if individual names were irrelevant in this compelling storm of creative empathy

Feelings

When I wake up in the morning
Sour hate,
This is the feeling inside me
Today,
It is like any other day
Unjust,
I hate the law that we obey
Disgust,
I see blood red as I'm waking
Thinking.
Thinking about the way we live
Pulsing
My blood runs fast through my veins
We've got to change it.

And back to Soweto in July 1976 and the blood of Hector Pietersen, the first of 600 young martyrs to be shot down by the apartheid police:

Hector

Lying on the ground.
Covered in dust
Blood on his mouth
Lying still
Very still.

Run and pick him up,
See if he breathes
Get him to safety
Cold and still
Very still.

Down on the ground,
His body is at peace
His mind is at rest
Peaceful and still
Very still.

Sheer eloquence in simplicity, becoming another in another
reality: as when Wally Mongane Serote wrote about his
own country's children, their language as 'simple of word':

From within mines and factories
From within mealie-fields, fruit orchards
and wheat fields they march
from within despicable ghettoes and villages
from out of the Bantustans and prisons
no longer with simplicity from ignorance
but they are simple of word
and so the little girls and boys
they emerge from out of an unripe youth
to mount the restless hour
they are freedom children.

I managed to contact Serote during a sojourn in London,
and he came to Sheffield and read his poems both in schools
and at the Caribbean cultural centre. I asked him to write
an introduction to the proposed *Freedom Children* – the
title was from his poem. His preface concluded:

*Of what significance are words, words, words, which are
meaningless, which have nothing to do with life, but are
just hot air? I would rather I learn from these children. I
would rather try to understand how they came to know
what they know, and what questions they asked themselves
to be able to say what they have said.*

*If they have not written poetry of words and words and
words which merely please the ear, and send us to sleep; if
they have not written poems which are hard to know what
they mean; if they have not written poems for the sake of
writing them, then, I am the first to read what they have
written. I am the first to call it poetry, for in these lines, life
is captured. I am told here, how to love life. Adults must
read these poems, and they must learn from these children.*

Perhaps he could have been writing about *Stepney Words,* about *Elders,* about the poems of the Basement Writers, about *Words Unchained,* or *Children of Steel,* for I have read nothing else that so describes them too, and little else that describes so wisely what, in truth poetry is about. *Freedom Children* had exemplified it, and from the heart of South Africa and its struggles, Serote had expressed it too.

The international solidarity so redolent in the poems of *Freedom Children* was a unique expression of young people's love across continents; the poetry of *Remember Hillsborough* of 1989 was a moving declaration of trans-Pennine love between three great British cities: Sheffield, Nottingham and Liverpool, provoked by the disaster at Hillsborough football ground in Sheffield at the FA Cup semi-final between Liverpool and Nottingham Forest on 15th of April 1989, when 96 Liverpool supporters were crushed to death and an additional 766 were injured.

I remember well walking up The Moor, Sheffield's main shopping street with my five-year-old son, Russell that same afternoon. We saw a large cluster of shoppers gathered outside a television rental shop, watching bewildered and horrified as the disaster happened before their eyes. It was an awakening nightmare as supporters grabbed advertising hoardings to carry their dying friends across the turf away from the deadly crush.

Remember Hillsborough

The Star

Following the tragedy many people turned to poetry; supporters, relatives of those who died, school children, those who could find no other way of setting down their shock and sorrow. As the poems came in to Sheffield City Council, to schools

Sheffield Town Hall; April 1990: Jabran Ishaq reads his poem at the launch of 'Remember Hillsborough'.

and local newspapers, a Liverpudlian staffing officer colleague in the Education Department Steve Chew and I decided to compile an anthology of them. We called it *Remember Hillsborough*. There were poems and prose pieces from all over the country, but mostly from Sheffield and Liverpool. Photographers from Sheffield newspapers provided images and the three managers of Liverpool, Nottingham Forest and Sheffield Wednesday: Kenny Dalglish, Brian Clough and Ron Atkinson all wrote introductory comments. 'Words can't replace anything especially lives,' wrote Clough: 'but they can help and I am delighted that this anthology is being produced by Sheffield City Council. It stands as a moving tribute to those who died and their love of football. *Remember Hillsborough* it's called – but there will never be a danger of it being forgotten'. The anthology's cover photograph showed a sumple bouquet attached to Hillsborough railings facing the pitch, with a couplet on a label attached to its ribbon:

Supporters of the world unite,
Rest in peace from Wednesdayites

The book's launch in the Town Hall's Mandela Room was a profoundly moving occasion. School children, footballers of Sheffield Wednesday – including club captain Nigel Pearson and grieving relatives read poems, and coachloads of Liverpool supporters came to Sheffield and an anonymous poem said exactly why:

The People of Steel

We've travelled from Anfield, the reason we came
Was to tell the people of Sheffield
That they were not to blame.

Tho' our homes and hearts were torn apart,
To thank you all – is so hard to start.

The kindness you showed to us,
On our bad day,
Will never be forgotten, forever,
Day by day.

So when you come to Liverpool
And we all pray you do
We'll welcome you with open arms
For 'Sheffield we love you'.

Six short lines of *Ken of Sheffield* became an apt and moving reply:

As the rose
That is plucked
Then crushed in the hand
Leaves a stain,
We bear the mask of their passing

One of the poems of *Remember Hillsborough* was called *Ode to a Gutter Reporter,* condemning the false reporting surrounding the tragedy and monstrously in the Murdoch tabloid *The Sun.* Liverpudlian poet Peggy Appleby wrote this in her poem, *Ode to a Gutter Reporter:*

Telling lies in big bold print
He piles on the dirt, he doesn't stint
Harassing mother, father and Gran
How can this creature look so like a man?

And a 15 year-old Sheffield schoolboy Julian Griffiths, wrote his brief and beautiful tribute:

The Flower that Fell

The flower that fell
for the man that fell
The petals that blew away
with the headlines

But the friends and memories
They won't blow away
Nor will they be seen or heard
The memories are all that's left
Of the people that fell to the ground

***

My time in Sheffield had not diminished my fervent interest in the literature of Africa, Latin America and the Caribbean. In September 1997, I met and interviewed for the *African Times* and the literary journal *Wasafiri*, the great Nigerian novelist Chinua Achebe, author of such momentous novels as *Things Fall Apart, No Longer at Ease, Arrow of God*, and *A Man of the People*. He had come to London to launch a new novel, *Anthills of the Savannah* and we met one afternoon at the flat where he was staying, near Bedford Square in West London. He spoke very passionately about what he called 'the bruised heart of Africa' and how his novel's theme was the persistence across the continent of many versions of neocolonialism. He called it 'a portmanteau word for all kinds of illnesses – colonialism coming back using local jokers as leaders'. It was the central question of true African leadership that concerned him most and how such leadership 'has to connect itself with the source of its legitimacy: the peasantry, the workers, the women – the people'. At the end of *Anthills of the Savannah* there is a kind of movement towards this reality.

For Achebe, the story itself was paramount. He told me: 'The story is more important than the writer, although they are related. Naturally. If you look at things that are happening in society: the struggle itself, the inspirer to struggle, the story of the struggle; when you put all these things together and say what is the most important, the choice falls upon the *story*. It is the *story* that conveys all our gains, all our failures and all we hold dear and all we condemn.'

His words made me think of Mozambique's late president Samora Machel, whose public speaking style emulated that of an animated, fervent and humorous African storyteller and who I had heard speak in both Nampula, Mozambique in 1977, and during his visit to Grenada in 1982. Achebe was insistent that African leadership must unite against South African apartheid, against famine, against hunger, against corruption. 'In Nigeria we do not have apartheid', he said, 'But the fact that the South African people are locked in this struggle diminishes us, and diminishes our own potential for solving our problems in Nigeria. For ultimately it is a struggle about the great wealth of South Africa and its economy and the way the wealth is *not used* for the benefit of Africa and its people. And of course the disruption it causes to other states in Africa like Mozambique for example.' And he spoke about South Africa's support for the anti-Frelimo, pro-South African forces in Mozambique's civil war. 'Mozambique cannot face its own problems of development because it has to constantly fight off the agents of South Africa. So the whole continent is one war front for anything that reduces an African in Ethiopia or South Africa reduces *all* Africans anywhere. So our writings must be political and must carry the vigour of those fundamental issues into it. There is not writing in Africa that can fail to be political.' These were lessons I had learned before and Achebe was reinforcing them again within me, like Machel had done in his speeches and story-telling brilliance.

Like the true African griot that he was Achebe kept referring to Machel, and I remembered his words in Nampula as our school was making an orchard in the space around its classrooms. On his visit he told us 'Plant the tree of Freedom everywhere!' Achebe added 'Despite the immense difficulties that Mozambique faces, these would have been infinitely worse without a leader like Machel or the same with Tanzania without a Nyerere. These are desperately poor countries yet they have never made a fiasco with independence. They have free education, which we don't have in Nigeria, even though they don't have oil. Machel is dead but actually he is not dead, and the same with Lumumba, Neto, Cabral and others. They stay in the memory of Africa, that is their greatest contribution. That we remember them and their struggle.' *Anthills of the Savannah* embodies these ideas in fiction and its characters and in the story it tells. Meeting and talking to Achebe only convinced me more that such ideas were central to any classroom work I would undertake in the future.

In 1989, in Sheffield, I met and interviewed El Salvador's great novelist Manlio Argueta, whose novel, *One Day of Life* I had read with my students in East London and used

Manlio Argueta.

as an impetus for their imaginative empathy and writing during a time when El Salvador's people were struggling against a US-backed dictatorship. Argueta reinforced in me how indivisible reading and writing are. In his own life as a novelist too. His novel about the history and living experience of the El Salvador peasantry, *Cuzcutlan* had recently been published. He called the people 'a gigantic family that has lived for over a thousand years'. I had reviewed *Cuzcutlan* in the *Caribbean Times*, and said about Argueta's writing that it is 'a prose that moves between outright realism and lyrical poetry, so that one minute he can be describing the experience of terrific suffering and the next he is telling of a young woman 'acquiring the grace of someone walking out of a cornfield ripened in the sun' or gently whispering to the reader 'to remember is to go and meet the shadows you once loved.' It is the seamlessly effortless motion between these opposites of life that makes Agueta's writing so compellingly beautiful. It could have been a novel about despair and the acceptance of pointless suffering if it hadn't been written by a revolutionary. It is a work of brilliance and struggle within which victory walks, expressing a people's unconquerable will towards freedom and the beauty they have carried through their history. 'We will survive despite our enemies. We were made of corn... we live here. It is our Land.'

I asked him how he had achieved the realism of portraiture of peasant life so critical in *One Day of Life* and *Cuzcutlan*. He told me it had involved thousands of hours of reading and listening to 'the tales and anecdotes of peasant life from real situations and above all to paint clearly the life of the peasants.' He said that only through these readings and living experiences could he gain his protagonists' 'sense of rebellion for a better life and vindicate their rights and democracy.' After learning this, he said it was possible to see that 'a new way appears, a perspective of looking for the methods to bring about a new life.' It was by living, reading and writing that this could be assured, hence the primacy of literacy campaigns that create new consciousness and changes. I still remember how perfectly he put it, and he made me feel that what I had learned in East London, Sheffield, in Mozambique, Canada and the Caribbean, were the results of the lessons I had been taught in these diverse places in the world, that there can never be any separation between reading, writing, living and educating. Such unity of method becomes the foundation of true critical literacy; truly the world is in our words, vibrant and potent in a new future.

I had developed a close relationship with SADACCA and organised a series of meetings there, inviting speakers, poets and writers mainly from London paid for by the Education Department. Poets like Jamaica's Elean Thomas, Grenada's Merle Collins or Trinidad's Brother Resistance. John Agard read his poems there and key historians like Barbados' Hilary Beckles (later to become vice-chancellor of the University of the West Indies) spoke on the theme of his book *Natural Rebels: A Social History of Enslaved Black Women in Barbados*. Richard Hart, Jamaican veteran griot and author of *Slaves who Abolished Slavery* introduced his book *Rise and Organise: The Birth of the Workers and National Movements in Jamaica*. They were always well-attended and responsive sessions.

I remember when Merle Collins read her extraordinary poem of colonial miseducation *The Lesson*, in which a Grenadian grandmother recounts all the British imperial history her school had taught her, some of the elderly Caribbean listeners were much affected by it. A veteran Jamaican SADACCA member rose from his seat and recited lines he had been compelled to learn at school, in Spanish Town, Jamaica, which he still remembered. He declaimed them with a sense of post-imperial amazement some seven decades on, in the heart of Sheffield, Yorkshire, England:

> Half Dominica leeward coast in 1782
> The valiant Rodney fought a fight
> That Frenchmen never ruled
> The fight that made Great Britain
> Chief among the Caribbees

He added that his grandchildren's brains must never be addled by such false and alienated knowledge. It was yet another cue for SUMES.

I was often helped in making contact with the speakers by my friend, the Tobago-born publisher, Buzz Johnson. I hadn't known Buzz in Tobago – he had been at school in Fyzabad, Southern Trinidad at the time, the hub of the rebellion of the then colony's oil workers in 1937, led by the storming Grenadian trade unionist Tubal Uriah 'Buzz' Butler, after whose sobriquet Buzz Johnson was informally named. I had met him in London, where we were both active in Liberation. Since those days, Buzz had become a prolific community publisher from his Hackney flat, and I had become a regular publicist and reviewer of his books. I could never work out how he managed to do it, because he had very little finance behind him, but between 1985 and 1991 he managed to publish more than thirty books, with minimal resources and little or no office or storage space, all under the imprint of Karia Press. And they were deeply significant publications too, from Merle Collins' poems *Because the Dawn Breaks* to his own book on the life and times of Claudia Jones, *'I think of My Mother'*, to transcripts of the Broadwater Farm and Liverpool 8 inquiries to Valentino O. Jones' *We are our own Educators: Josina Machel School, from Supplementary to Black Complementary School*. He also republished Bernard Coard's seminal text: *How the West Indian Child is Made Educationally Subnormal in the British School System* and Young World Books' *Tales of Mozambique*. He put two of my books into print too, my memoir of the Revo, which I called *Grenada Morning* and my account of the Ethiopian Literacy Campaign, *A Blindfold Removed*. Buzz often came up to Sheffield too, and on one of his sojourns he heard a young Zimbabwean university student called Chisiya read tales of his people to primary school children in Pitsmoor, Sheffield's most multiracial neighbourhood. Moved and impressed, he published these stories as *Afrikan Lullaby: Folk Tales from Zimbabwe*. This typified his approach to publishing.

Buzz was truly a people's publisher. When he died in 2014, Hackney and many places and people beyond whose

106

words had found print in Karia Press and whom he had directly through his compassion and militancy, remembered him with love and respect from Port of Spain to Namibia, from Stoke Newington to Belize. I thought of the beauty and fire of the people from his Tobago birthplace and the words of Buzz Butler, from whom he took his name. They were the words of his bloodstream and his living spirit.

> There is no power, no bribe, to make me turn aside from the paths of truth and beauty and freedom. Beauty and freedom and all that these contain fall not like ripened fruit about our feet. We climb to them through years of sweat and pain; without life's struggles none do ye attain! We must all struggle and keep struggling until the goals of truth, freedom, beauty and liberty are reached.

***

By 1990, I had been working in Sheffield Education Department for six years, and decided it was time to move on. SUMES was now a large-scale educational enterprise with upwards of 160 posts in many diverse contexts, and Ahmed's determined and creative stewardship had made it a powerful force within the LEA. I started making applications for posts outside Sheffield, and was interviewed for headships in Derby and Haringey, for a professorship in Education at Newcastle and for the Chief Adviser's post on the familiar ground of Waltham Forest, East London. As it transpired, in May 1990 I was also due to be interviewed for two headships in Sheffield; Earl Marshal and Abbeydale Grange Schools. Earl Marshal came first, and I was offered the post. I took it happily – I'd been general adviser to the school for five years, so knew some of its staff, as well as knowing some of its problems. I was told much later that the day after my appointment was made public, Bill Walton received a phone call from the Department of Education and Science in London that my appointment should not be confirmed, but should be rescinded. Bill apparently told the official that the appointment process had been done with complete correctness, (he had been on the appointment panel) and that there was no reason whatsoever that it should not be confirmed in the normal way. I didn't know about this for many years, but I suppose that had I known, I shouldn't have been surprised, neither at the government's reaction or Bill Walton's resolve and bravery. When we received the encouragement and financial contribution from the Chief Education Officer of the West Riding of Yorkshire, Sir Alec Clegg in 1971 for our publishing of *Stepney Words* in East London, I never thought I would ever be directly grateful to another Yorkshire CEO in Sheffield some two decades on for supporting me again. This time it was Bill Walton, and I have never forgotten his courage and integrity or his commitment to racial justice.

Chapter 4
A School of the World

Earl Marshal School was a school of many contradictions. Its name had an aristocratic ring to it: the 'Earl Marshal' of England was a hereditary royal officeholder with a chivalric title, bestowed by the sovereign to the Duke of Norfolk, holder of one of the country's richest dukedoms, with the ownership of land and enterprises in Sheffield, among many other places in England. And this was a school serving some of the poorest and most struggling neighbourhoods in Sheffield: Pitsmoor, Fir Vale, Burngreave, Page Hall and Grimesthorpe. Yet it was also one of the culturally richest catchment areas in the city. The largest section of its school population were families from the Mirpur region of Pakistan and Kashmir, with other strong communities with their roots in Yemen, the Caribbean and Northern Somalia – at the time re-defining itself as the internationally unrecognised 'Somaliland' – from where many young Somali refugees and their families had arrived from 1989 onward, escaping from government violence and repression in the Civil War in cities like Hargeisa and Burao. There was another minority of local white children. Many of the fathers and grandfathers of these children had worked in the steel industry, frequently as with the Yemenis, in the lowest and most dangerous rungs of employment, and the Don Valley industrial graveyard was very close. There were also children at the school from Nigeria, Ethiopia, Brunei, Syria and Bangladesh. It was indeed a school of the world and I was determined to teach as full a timetable as I could. Remembering Picasso in Sheffield in 1950, I chose a new symbol to replace the Duke of Norfolk's heraldic lions on the school badge: three doves, black, white and brown soaring from an open book, with the watchwords: 'For

109

Excellence and Community.' Under the crest were Bob Marley's words from the lyrics of his *Redemption Song*: 'None but ourselves can free our minds.'

As for the teachers, they were an amalgam too. Some of the most progressive and creative colleagues I would ever work with taught at the school, alongside some of the most authoritarian and backward-looking. There were, for example, three ex-police officers among the teachers, one of whom was a Deputy Head who had also been interviewed for the headship. After I was appointed I said to him that I hoped that we could enjoy a positive relationship together in leading the school. His response was at least very clear: 'I don't agree with your ideas, or your politics; I don't think that's possible.' It was a prophetic enough rejoinder.

The school was unstreamed, non-uniform and physically very much a part of its own community. It had no fences or divisive walls; and a path across its campus was used as a shortcut by local residents walking between Owler Lane and Earl Marshal Road. It passed next to the school entrance lobby. Within its grounds were both a youth club which opened every day and was well-used at lunchtimes by the students; and a sports centre, used by the school yet open to the community in the evenings, where we would in time establish our cricket centre. There were also tarmacked football pitches which were full of sporting life every evening. The school grounds were sometimes abused with occasional burnt-out cars and discarded syringes and other evidence of drug use. Two twelve year old girls were to write poems emblematising this forbidding aspect of campus reality. Sarah and Shama pulled no punches:

The Syringe

I am the syringe
That you find in the street.
I am the syringe
that attacks you on the waste ground.
I am the syringe
That pricks you and kills you.

110

I am the syringe
that you should stay away from!

I am like a live snake
that gives you a bite.
I am like a live wire
that gives you a shock.

Stay away!
Or else you will have
a very short time to live.

What does it feel like
when you leave your child
standing on the waste ground
and I prick her ?
What would you do
when your child is infected?
What would you do?

The Needle

The needle
that was lying on the floor.
The needle
that was calling me more and more.
The needle
that shone in my eye.
The needle
that convinced me
not to live but to die.
The needle
that gives me pain.
The needle
that turns me insane.
The needle
which will never let me
be a good wife
The needle which has taken
over my life!

The teachers were divided between two major unions. The
largest group were members of the National Association of
Schoolmasters/Union of Women Teachers, which at the

time often took authoritarian positions on school life, had few Black members and under the direction of their General Secretary, Nigel de Gruchy, were pressing hard for schools to exclude more students, which they saw as a strategy for keeping 'better discipline.' The other main group were members of the National Union of Teachers, of which I was still, even though I had been an adviser, a committed and active member, although I decided as headteacher, not to involve myself in school union affairs as I thought it might inhibit the actions and arguments of teacher members. I was massively grateful to the NUT, which between 1971 and 1973 had fought hard and successfully for my reinstatement as a teacher in Sir John Cass and Redcoat school in Stepney, East London, after I had been sacked in May 1971 for publishing my students' poems in *Stepney Words*.

My first dispute with the NAS/UWT came soon after I started at Earl Marshal, in October 1990. I had been in post for just over a month when a group of senior boys came to my office and asked to speak to me. One of them, a Pakistani boy, complained that his form teacher (who was also the school representative of the NAS/UWT, whom I shall call 'Mr N'), had called him in class, a 'Dickhead' and a 'Plonkbrain.' The other four boys were white, and they gave him their complete support, and were also angry that one of their girl classmates had been called a 'silly bitch' by Mr N in the same registration. When I discussed the meeting with the Deputy Head, he told me that senior boys were worried that the same teacher had been becoming 'too familiar' with some of the senior girls.

The next day, I spoke with Mr N, a middle-aged Craft, Design and Technology (CDT) teacher. Medallions swung from around his neck, over his shirt's open buttons. He admitted to the insults, which he said were due to the stress of rushing back for morning registration after a preschool briefing I had given to the teachers. He said that he had lost his temper and would apologise to the class members involved. Later in the day, he came to my office and said that he wanted to refute the allegations about over-familiarity with girl students and that the nickname 'Mr Pervert' which had been affixed to him was completely unwarranted. The accusations kept coming. His head of department said that he had warned him about his behaviour with girl students many times and that he had often been worried about his isolation from the rest of the department, teaching in a prefabricated building at the extreme end of the campus with his own room which had a small bed in it. Several women teachers, both middle-aged and young came forward to complain about Mr N's offensive physicality to them in the past, and how girl students had spoken to them worriedly and nervously about the teacher's actions. A white girl said he had been sidling up to her and other students in lessons, rubbing up against them and touching their bottoms. A Pakistani girl accompanied by a woman teacher demonstrated how he regularly winked and leered at her, and put his arms over her shoulders and the upper part of her body. She, like many of her friends, was worried sick about the consequences for her if her parents ever found out.

It was clear that a full investigation needed to be done, and I remember how shocked I felt that one had not been done before, as teachers were quite clear that this behaviour had been going on for years (one ex-staff member said as long ago as 1972) and had been endured by both women staff and students. I rang up the Education Department, told an Education Officer what had transpired, and was advised to temporarily suspend Mr N pending a full and proper investigation. As headteacher, he told me, I would need to be Investigating Officer.

I asked several women teachers to interview around twenty girls, most of whom were fifteen or sixteen years old. The girls were asked to write down what had happened to them, and I was shocked by what they wrote. They described how he frequently touched their breasts and bottoms from the second year onward: 'I thought he might have stopped, but he didn't, he started again, he made me feel sick,' wrote one. Others said how they had truanted his classes because they were so disgusted with him: 'I didn't want to come to school on Wednesdays because of him.' Others wrote of their fear of telling other teachers about him because 'I thought they would not believe me.' Another said: 'I didn't think anyone would take any notice of me because he's a teacher and I'm only a child.' The girls had clearly suffered hugely. 'I felt sick inside,' wrote one: 'I felt cold, sick and uncomfortable,' attested another. 'For eight weeks I didn't come to school because every time I used to turn up to his lessons he used to act weird and put his arms around me in front of all the class and put his hands where I didn't like it.' It wasn't easy for them to write these things, and the Muslim girls were especially distraught. Some were worried that if their parents ever found out what had happened in Mr N's classes, they would be sent permanently to Pakistan.

The hearing was held in the LEA offices, now without Bill Walton, who had retired. Mr N was represented by the Regional Officer of his union, who clearly saw me as the enemy and the instigator of all this trouble for his member. In a recess he said to one of the education officers: 'I don't know what all the fuss is about. It's only a problem if anything happens inside the clothing.' When the written statements of the girls were put before the panel they were finally discounted and annulled because the girls couldn't remember the exact dates when the incidents happened. How could they? These events had been going on for two or three years of their school lives, from the second year to the fifth year. Their evidence was dismissed, with the Labour cabinet member for education in the chair. I couldn't believe it, neither could I conceive how the evidence and emotions of children could be treated with so much disdain and disrespect by a Labour education department too, and one for whom I had worked diligently for six years.

I left the Education Department after the late afternoon decision and went straight over the road, Leopold Street, to the Town Hall and asked to see officers of the Children's

Department. I gave them copies of all the papers of the case and the girls' evidence. The Children's Department representatives were as shocked as I was, and immediately contacted the National Society for the Prevention of Cruelty to Children and the South Yorkshire Police. I didn't want that outcome because I trusted that the LEA would truly act on the girls' evidence and suffering rather than preferring their sweetheart relationship with the NAS/UWT, but I had no choice. But I knew that I had made two new and serious enemies, the Local Education Authority itself, and the larger of the two unions in the school. So the future wasn't going to be easy. But thankfully, Mr N never came back to the school, so at least many of its girls could breathe more freely and study more readily.

But my first term at Earl Marshal wasn't all conflict. It ended with a felicitous event, the visit of the captain of the Pakistan cricket team that in 1992 was to win the World Cup, Imran Khan, to the school. He was trying to raise money to build a cancer hospital in Lahore, in memory of his mother who had died from the disease. As soon as I'd

Imran Khan at
Earl Marshal
School,
December 1990.

115

got his promise of a visit, students began fundraising in the community, and a lot of money was raised. He arrived one Sunday afternoon in December, and a huge reception awaited him as Pakistani families and other curious local residents turned out, over a thousand local people, to welcome him. We set up the cricket nets in the sports hall, and he bowled the first balls of what would become the school's cricket centre. Of course, none of those who were there knew that in 2018 he was to become his nation's Prime Minister.

If there was one truth which I had learned, working and teaching in the heart of revolutionary education systems in both Mozambique and Grenada, it was the power and all the educational insights and progress that were provoked in community self-organising and mass mobilising. Even as I came in every day to work at Earl Marshal, I remembered the Grenadian calypso that Mighty Awful used to sing:

We are free at last
Not as in the past -
Forward ever!
Backward never!
Mass mobilisation
Pushing the struggle on!
Who trying, trying in vain,
Nothing cannot stop
The freedom train!

Strange perhaps, for a white Englishman to be silently singing and thinking these lyrics on the bus going to the heart of Fir Vale, Sheffield, Yorkshire, England, but such were the words which were rushing around in my head every morning.

Organising for the Imran Khan visit and the mass local response that it set in motion reminded me of Mozambican and Grenadian days, but it also showed me what this community could do, if given the encouragement and reason to self-organise. In 1997, a year after I left Earl Marshal, I wrote a book called *Living Community, Living School*. I tried to set out this approach to education. Of course, it was the contrary to everything OFSTED and the government said that inner city schools should do. To me it seemed obvious that the more you raised activism around the purposes and functions of community needs and improvement, the more you raised the motivation to learn: it was what Fanon had called 'actional education,' and I knew how imperative it had been in Mozambique and Grenada – and in Stepney and Poplar too in a previous East London life: communities learn when they have something to learn for, that can improve their lives. One particular review in the *New Statesman* of *Living Community, Living School* surprised me. It was written by Tim Brighouse, the Chief Education Officer of England's second city, Birmingham, and an educational administrator close to the progressive mould of Alec Clegg and Bill Walton. He wrote: 'This collection of essays reminds one of several perennial issues, especially the need for remarkable energy to inspire excellence in the inner city. So much of what Searle did at Earl Marshal is remarkable in the sense that he had the chance to do it. For those who appointed him must have known, since he was an adviser in Sheffield and since his career was 'in their faces,' that he would take the radical steps he did. Here was a throwback revolutionary taken on in a school written off for closure in a post-Baker education world where competition was going to be driven by league tables in an unforgiving market place.'

He was right: the clash of educational ideas and practices could not have been sharper.

Debates around schools and their rationales were largely overtaken in January 1991 with the start of Operation Desert Storm, a US-led military operation to expel occupying Iraqi forces from Kuwait. For Earl Marshal students this was no faraway conflict. Many of their families, particularly those of the Arab students, felt deeply and emotionally involved. During the period when the conflict was at its most intense, the school could have become a venue for ructions but instead became a venue of intense

117

debate and creative output, with assemblies and classes and a contested parents meeting, all trying to find a unified way through the discord. Students wrote poems, essays, stories and political accounts putting different sides of the arguments for war, and the school itself became a parliament of youth, with essential differences being openly aired, but never descending to threats, clashes or feuds. The school was coming to terms with real antagonisms in a non-violent and peaceful ambiance, and much powerful student writing and debate emanated from it. I tried to describe and detail it in an essay, *The Gulf Between: A School and a War*, which was published in *Race & Class* and later in *Living Community, Living School*. It proved to me that the school could contain, encourage and promote difference, for difference and diversity were essential to its very being. As one sixteen year old Yemeni boy, Mohammed, wrote about 'the powers that be' that fomented the conflict and the students in the school who overcame it:

> They want to rule what is not theirs,
> They make excuses and support millionaires.
> If only they could stop and think on their demands,
> Maybe war would stop and they could shake hands.
> Peace could stop killing in the sand.
> Peace could remove the gun from the hand.
> Solidarity is the way we should live today,
> And together as one we should stand up for our say.

***

It wasn't long before the students and parents had another prime opportunity to 'stand up for our say.' In February 1991 in its *Schools Review*, Sheffield Education Department decided that it needed to close secondary schools, in particular those which had a problem of 'viability' because they were considered too small to properly deliver the National Curriculum which had been conceived as an absolute necessity following the 1988 Education Act. It was considered that the closure of either Earl Marshal or another local secondary school, Herries, 'would assist the financial viability of neighbouring schools.' The *Schools Review* was a profoundly bureaucratic and anti-democratic process, and teachers, parents and school communities had no opportunity for either consultation or alternative proposals. When I suggested in a letter to a senior education officer that it was little more than a compendium of 'broom cupboard' proposals, such criticisms were not happily received. It was also a harmful 'divide and rule' proposal that the head of Herries, a genial Liverpudlian called Graham Evans, (who I knew well professionally as I had been Herries' general adviser) and I decided to oppose by adopting a position of unity. Neither of the schools should be closed, we declared together and in solidarity, both were too precious to their communities.

Earl Marshal students, parents and teachers thought so too, and began an intense community-based campaign to save both schools which served very different communities – Herries was on the mostly white Shirecliffe estate – but both were thoroughly working class schools. As for the communities served by Earl Marshal, there was a burgeoning unity developing during the course of the campaign to save the school, which had begun with the Yemenis and Pakistanis running their own separate campaigns, but this soon changed as they created a joint strategy. Within the Yemeni ranks too there were significant changes happening. Abdulgalil Shaif, a Yemeni governor, told the Sheffield *Star* after a large picket was organised by Yemeni men and women outside the school gates during a visit by a councillor:

> It is the first time men and women have picketed together like this, and it shows the strength of feeling within the community. They see this as just the start of the fight. If the school closes they will lose twenty years of struggle to get the facilities they have today.

For the Yemenis, the school had a particular preciousness because it was now the free venue of a weekend Arabic-medium supplementary and language school. They were

119

Yemenis defend Earl Marshal School, 1991.
photo:Sheffield Newspapers Ltd.

determined not to lose it. Another governor, Lambert
Poyser from the Pitsmoor African-Caribbean community,
was determined that the school should be saved for his
community too, and told the *Star*: 'I have knocked on doors
and talked to a lot of people about education – something I
would not normally do. Everyone has been cooperative and
Afro-Caribbean families are being drawn back to the
school. A few years ago it seemed to me they weren't interested in Earl Marshal, but not now they see what's
happening there and are attracted back.'

As for the students, even for some of those most alienated
and estranged from school life and study, the school became
as a magnet for them. They made banners, wrote and
recorded songs and tapes, took part in demonstrations and
composed poems in their English lessons. A tape circulated
the shops and streets of Fir Vale with a song directed to the
Education Department called *What'cha Ting Ya Doin?* on
one side, with another by two Pakistani girls called *Save
our School* on the flipside, the result of a song competition
launched by the music teacher.

With such an outpouring of community-inspired protest, there was no way that the LEA could close either school. Both were reprieved, with the Education Department admitting that support for both schools was impossible to ignore. A culture of resistance had been generated, and as I tried to express it in an article that I wrote for *Race & Class* called *Campaigning is Education*, the beginnings of actional education at the school. As Marie had expressed it so succinctly in her poem; written on victory day:

> Today's the day
> Our good news reigns,
> You people here
> Have taken pains
> To save our school,
> And see it shine.
> 'Can't stop us now
> We're in our prime!'

***

During 1991 a large number of Somali young people were arriving in Sheffield as refugees from the civil war, and many families settled in the neighbourhoods around the school. Few of them could speak any English at all. Some of them were young men who were clearly older than school age, but we still welcomed them to the school so we could teach them English. Several of the boys had been on the fringes of military groups and some of them were still dealing with the lasting effects of war wounds. When one boy appeared, limping on crutches and clearly in pain, we took him to the accident and emergency department of the nearby Northern General Hospital, and a bullet was discovered, still festering in his thigh. The other students and teachers knew nothing about why their new classmates sought refuge in Sheffield, so we devised a 'Somali Fortnight,' in which we organised a series of events that would teach the school about Somalia, its recent history and the real life experiences of our newest students. For the Somali girls, many of them had excruciating experiences

121

which they needed to tell: like Nabat, whose horrific odyssey shocked all who read it:

When I was a little girl I used to go to the mosque to read the Koran and learn about Islam. The mosque was big and beautiful and had flowers, red, yellow and orange flowers over it. I never went to school. When I was eight I used to stay at home and look after my younger brother Ahmed and feed him, while my mother went to the market to work. She sold potato, onion and tomato and also some clothes.

Then the war came to my town Burao and it was like a slaughterhouse. Wherever you looked you saw dead people – women, children and the old ones. The houses were all knocked down and bombed. There were hardly any walls or roofs, and big holes were everywhere. People were blown up by mines sometimes, and they lost their legs and feet. The side of my body was burned and scarred by a fire from a bomb. All the lights were out at night, it was all dark. You could only see people's eyes gleaming. It was frightening for us, like a long long night that was never going to end. The government soldiers came into our houses and killed the men and whipped and raped the women. They swore at us, using terrible words. They took my cousin Farah who was 22 and they cut his arm across the wrists and they made us watch him when they killed him. All of us were crying, we never stopped crying. They said to us, 'if you go, we're going to kill you!' Then they raped his wife. All this I can never forget. I still dream about it, then I wake up from my sleep and I am shouting. I still hear the bazookas and the explosions as the shells hit our houses.

Then one day we decided that we must move from there and then come back when the war was finished. So me, my mother, my little brother, my uncle and other friends set off walking out of our city. We walked and walked out into the country. We just hoped we would leave Somalia and go into Ethiopia. On our journey we passed sheep and people on donkeys and camels. It was rocky and sandy and at nights we made a fire. We had to watch out for wild animals and snakes. Once, when I picked up a piece of wood for a fire, a long snake was there and it bit me on the finger. Someone cut the head off the snake and something was put on my finger to heal it, but it never got well and is still bent and doesn't go straight. The soldiers came after us and once we saw a pregnant woman who had been killed by them. At nights we just used to lie down on the ground to sleep, that was our bed.

We stayed some time with a farmer. He was good to us and gave us some of his food. Then we were lucky to get a ride on a truck that was going to Diredawa. This truck was so full that you could hardly move your hands or feet. But the driver was a good man. He stopped by us and said, 'we can take you to Ethiopia.' But it was so tight with everyone on the truck. One woman and her baby were crushed as they had no room to breathe. Once when we were off the truck I fell down and couldn't get up, I was so thirsty. But my mother picked me up and told me: 'We've got to keep going! Keep going! Remember the soldiers are behind us!' I learned on that journey that you could bear anything for peace.

When we came to the camp at Daroor in Ethiopia, thousands of people were just sleeping on the ground and a lot of people died. For food we only had mashaali, a kind of brown flour meal. But at least, for a little while we felt we were safe, even here where there was no clean water and so many diseases.

Then my grandmother arrived and she had visas for England for us. We were so happy to see her. We couldn't stop hugging and kissing her. She thought that we had all been killed so she was crying too to see us alive. So through her we came to get out of that hell! We went to Diredawa and Addis Ababa by bus, then to Moscow, then to London and then to Sheffield. We just looked everywhere, we'd never seen so many white people before. Grandmother said to us 'come on, don't look at the people all the time!' We were just looking, looking, looking, – and looking at the buildings too. We only had old clothes to wear, just the ones we had before, but all the Somalis in Sheffield helped us so they gave us some money and we bought some new English clothes.

Now when I remember, I still miss my friends in my city of Burao. I know many of them have died, but I still dream here in Sheffield of my old life in Somalia, and perhaps, one day, I will make another journey and go back there.

Many children told of similar long, long journeys. One boy, Moqtar, had the idea of symbolically re-enacting the Somali odyssey on Wincobank Hill, behind the school, a rounded grassy crest where during the Roman invasion,

Moqtar's journey on Wincobank Hill.

local Brigante warriors had held off the might of the Roman army in a long siege. Signs of different key points: Burao, Hargeisa, Diredawa in one direction, Djibouti in another, Addis Ababa, Moscow, London and Sheffield were posted at various points on the hill, and the students had to track their way. There was a parents' evening where the Somalis' story was told, a long article in the Sheffield *Star* was written by members and parents of the Somali Community Association and a Somali football team, reinforced by Yemeni players, was established. A beautiful cloth Somali banner was made with the school's watchwords: 'For excellence and community' in Somali woven onto a mauve background with the school's three doves, black, white and brown, flying from it. The 'Somali Fortnight' established an exemplar. Later we emulated it with similar series of events celebrating and educating the school about its very own communities, with weeks dedicated to the histories, cultures, artifacts and realities of Yemen, then Kashmir.

For fourteen year old Zulfiqar, the Kashmir attachment was very strong, and the exhibition about his family's motherland had a special resonance: 'It's a life issue,' he said to the *Star* journalist. His poem expressed that closeness with a particular eloquence:

Beauty and Death in Kashmir

Kashmir, Kashmir!
What should I say about Kashmir?
Shall I talk about the poverty
Or shall I talk about the beauty?
The mountains sparkling
The rivers flowing,
What shall I say?
People dying
Mothers crying
What shall I say?
Pakistan and India fighting
Over this beautiful place,
What shall I say?
Snowtops on the mountains
Forests on the sides of rivers,
What shall I say?
Innocent people are *dying,*
And those who are dead lay there
In these beautiful mountains
In these riverine places,
What shall I say?
Forts on the ends
Of carpets of corn,
What shall I say?
What will become of this place
If the fighting goes on?
What shall I say?
The rivers will flow
The mountains will die
But the dying will die.
The beauty may go
If this fighting does not stop –
Kashmir, Kashmir!
What should I say about
Kashmir?

The mobilising factor of self-organisation as a motivating element of the school's students was distrusted by some teachers but particularly strong among the girls, and was prompted around the Imran Khan visit and the quest to raise money for the Lahore cancer hospital. The fundraising energy in local shops and businesses was truly impressive, as was the pride of the students in what they were doing. The *Star* published a moving story of several of the girls visiting local care homes, giving their cricket-loving, mostly white residents, autographed posters of the world-renowned cricketer. A few weeks on and another press story told of a gift to a group of girls of a beautifully sequined framed Koranic tapestry, given to the girls at the end of the Gulf War. The givers had been Iraqi university students in Sheffield, whose families had been helped by food and money collected by the Earl Marshal girls, after the students' money from their home country had ceased on

Iraqi's peace gift for school

the outbreak of war. It was as if the power of raising funds and giving had been set free, for it never stopped, and became a major feature of school life for the next five years. Sawsan, from Jordan, told the *Star*: 'They are normal people like us, but have nothing to live on. They don't qualify for any British benefits.' And her friend Kay added: 'It's important that we do something to help. We visited one family and the way they were living is appalling. They are struggling just to get food.'

A major and more far-away resource project grew out of Somali Fortnight, with hundreds of the younger students raising funds to equip new schools in Burao and Hargeisa in Northern Somalia – cities that the students had suddenly learned about on their own senses through the 'Fortnight.' Asma, from a Bangladeshi family wrote about 'another kind of war,' a war against racism in Britain that many Somali families faced. And this after the terrifying suffering in the place they had arrived from:

I still remember what yesterday's horror brought,
The blood that stained the earth
And the blood that stained streets.
The bodies that were twisted
And bodies that were bent –
That was the evil soul of men.
The eyes did not see a death that was clear.
Tears in my eyes, tears of pain.

Our land once grew a sweet kind of fruit
But now only sour bullets will grow.
The streams and the rivers only flow blood.
The massive garden of flowers
Has now died away.
Our homes have been burnt to ashes –
Tears in my eyes, tears of my land.

And I thought of my Bangladeshi students in East London, and how they had arrived in Stepney and Poplar in the early seventies with similar memories of their homeland and often similar stories of a grim welcome in London.

As soon as the students heard about the situation of the Kurds in Iraq after the Gulf War, they went at it again. They raised money for medical supplies, and when a Kurdish doctor, Razgar Amin, came to thank the students during an assembly, he told them that the Kurds always saw their only real friends as the mountains of their country, but that now they realised that they also had good friends at Earl Marshal School. The students listened hard and were deeply moved. Some of the girls heard about the plight of refugees from Bosnia. They went straight into a frenzy of cake-baking and selling to raise funds for them.

In early 1993 Pakistan was assailed by serious floods, some of them directly affecting the families of our students. Already in the habits of fundraising and campaigning, the students mobilised themselves and their communities again for a strong effort. A fourteen year old girl, Shameem, had her poem published in the Sheffield *Gazette*:

The rains brought the flood,
My eyes brought a tear,
Death lingered over my people
I can't hide my fear.

Pakistan flooded,
A thousand dead
I cry my heart out,
Be patient, they said.

I'm not going to stand helpless
Neither should you.
Help them, help my people,
Now they need us, it's true.

Stop those tears,
Don't waste your time crying,
Be brave like me,
Stop our people from dying.

Give with food, give with money,
If you've nothing to offer, just pray,
But don't stand there doing nothing,
We need you today.

It was like a call to arms across the newspapers of Sheffield as well as the consciousnesses of Fir Vale. It was also an expression of how so many of our students saw learning and action as indivisible.

Many first year students responded to a call from another continent, when in 1992 a cholera epidemic broke out in Guyana. They raised funds for medical supplies and received a letter of thanks from the nation's president, Dr. Cheddi Jagan. He wrote, under the embossed presidential crest: 'I have been deeply moved by the concern and personal efforts displayed by the first year pupils of Earl Marshal Comprehensive School. This demonstration of unity and individual involvement reflects positively for future generations. Their example will inspire others, and will no doubt be duplicated. Relatives of persons affected by cholera and the victims who have benefited from the efforts of these youths, I am sure, will ever be grateful to them.'

The generosity and internationalism that drove these actions had a home front too, and the students were not reticent to involve themselves in the heart of it. When they heard about the racist attack on the Bangladeshi youth Quddus Ali in a street in Whitechapel, East London, in 1993 and the arrest of the 'Tower Hamlets Nine' at a vigil organised to protest against the attack, the Earl Marshal students were inspired to write many poems and prose pieces in solidarity with the nine young people, like themselves, who had been locked up, and of course, Quddus himself, who was still in a coma in a hospital bed. The school invited members of the Tower Hamlets Nine Defence Committee to a community meeting at the school, and many parents too were shocked at what had happened to Quddus. Students read their poems at this meeting, and Farooq's entitled, *Quddus and the Nine*, carried a particular power:

> He is lying there like a dead body
> Trying to fight for his life.
> He knows what's happening outside
> He can feel the pain over and over again

129

Like a bad nightmare.
His friends are opening a campaign
To fight for their rights
To defend themselves and their families.
Then the police came,
Hitting whoever came in their way.
Nine teenagers were arrested
And all they did was defend themselves.
Quddus is still in hospital
And if he dies
And if the nine go to prison,
Then there will be no such word
As JUSTICE!

EDUCATION REPORT

Campaign that captured students' imagination: Nageeb Hussain (left) Abida Begum and Ghulam Farooq were three of the pupils at the protest meeting

Freedom fight

STUDENTS at Sheffield's Earl Marshal School have joined the fight to free nine Asians said to have been unjustly arrested in an anti-racism demonstration.

Pupils met members of the campaign to free the Tower Hamlets Nine, who were arrested during a vigil staged to protest against the brutal beating of a Bangladeshi teenager.

"The lad was in a coma for three months and feelings in the East End were running very high," explained headteacher Chris Searle.

Project

"Then came the vigil and these arrests which served to inflame the situation still further.

"Students had been doing project work on racism and this story really caught their imagination. So members of the campaign were invited up to give us a first hand account."

Around 100 parents, students and members of the local community attended a later public meeting in which pupils read poetry and voiced their own opposition to racist attacks.

Support for Quddus and the Tower Hamlets Nine.

130

Two hundred miles apart were these youths of London and Sheffield, yet that night their mutual empathy was total. Two days later I received a letter from the campaign organisers describing our students' poems as 'really beautiful and very moving... giving us hope and inspiration to continue this struggle... a ray of sunshine in what can sometimes be a very bleak landscape.' A few weeks later, when local police arrested a group of Sheffield Asian youths who were preparing to defend themselves from racist attacks on the streets of Darnall, Sheffield, several of our students were on a vigil *Outside Attercliffe Police Station,* the title of Sadakat's poem:

Everyone was there last night at the picket,
Fighting for their brothers
Fighting for their freedom
Fighting for their religion
Fighting against racism
Fighting against the whole of Attercliffe Police Station,
For their brothers who were arrested for nothing.
I was feeling strong to see my younger brothers there,
Fighting against the racist people jumping up and down,
Up and down
For their younger brothers,
And on the flag it said
NO JUSTICE, NO PEACE!
It took a lot of strength to hold those flags
In such a windy place like Attercliffe.
That's what I saw last night,
And I was there too!

So was I, and the way Sadakat described the scene was full of truth.

Another 'actional' event took place towards the end of the football season in 1992. Coach loads of supporters of Sunderland Football Club took a shortcut from the M1 to Hillsborough football ground through Fir Vale to watch their club play Sheffield Wednesday. They jeered at local residents, calling out racist insults and left a trail of abuse as they passed. One of our fifth year students, Asma, was writing up a short dissertation on racism at the time. She contacted fans in Sunderland through their local fanzine *A Love Supreme* and wrote to its editor about the events. The fanzine exposed the racism among the supporters in Sunderland, and the club manager, Malcolm Crosby wrote a letter of apology to the school, asking to pass his sentiments on to local people. It all created publicity in the Sheffield press and gave a sense of pride and relief to students at the school. In a small but significant way, their protest had created change.

Shock findings of survey on racism

RACISM is still a problem in Sheffield despite a growing awareness of other cultures, claims schoolgirl Asma Bibi.

And schools are being urged to overcome racism by steering children away from prejudice.

Fifteen-year-old Asma carried out a survey in the north of the city — and was stunned at the extent of racial abuse reported.

She said: "I sent out 60 questionnaires and every one was returned to me. Only four people had never experienced racism.

"I was amazed — I thought people probably understood each other better now.

Certainly at school we do a lot of work on race and all the community groups get on well together."

Asma — who came to Sheffield from Bangladesh in 1980 — did the survey as part of her Humanities work at Earl Marshal School, Fir Vale. She had replies from Bangladeshi, Pakistani, Arab, Afro Caribbean, Somali, Indian, half-cast Irish, French, Polish and Spanish people and white people in mixed marriages.

She explained: "Mostly we can only read about racism in books by professional researchers, but I wanted to find out how Sheffield people really feel about it."

Asma found that:
● Most people had suffered harrassment in the street, though others had been abused in or near their own homes or on public transport;
● More than half the respondents had been insulted by strangers but pupils, neighbours and work colleagues had also occasionally given abuse;
● Most harrassment was carried out by groups of two to five people. No one said they had been abused by a single person;
● Men were more likely to give racist insults than women;
● Arranged marriages, religion and lifestyle were often the subject of abuse;
● Most children did not tell their parents they had been harrassed, mostly because they were too embarrassed or did not want to worry them.

Earl Marshal pupil Asma Bibi with her survey on racism

Asma's campaign

***

Student-led changes in the heart of the school began to have an impact. In early 1994 a group of Pakistani girls came to see me with a very positive idea. They wanted to open a breakfast club in the school's main lobby, to cater for the increasing number of students who were arriving at school in the mornings without having eaten. They told me that they saw this as a serious problem, threatening many students' ability to study. Named after one of the girls, 'Shaheen's Cafe' proved to be a real early morning success.

Pupils flock for breakfast treats

By Mike Russell,
EDUCATION CORRESPONDENT

WELCOME to Shaheen's . . . .

It's the perfect place for an early morning brew and a bite to eat. The regulars are friendly and the staff are quick with a smile and a cheery hello.

But this is a breakfast club with a difference — it's run by students at Earl Marshal School and to fellow pupils the morning menu is absolutely free!

In the few weeks since its launch Shaheen's — named after one of the organisers, 15-year-old Shaheen Akhtar — has proved to be a big hit.

"A lot of people don't get any breakfast at home so there's been plenty of demand," explained Dill Afroz, also 15.

The menu's simple — tea, coffee,

> The five girls who run it have to be keen to be in early each day to warm up the toaster and prepare the kettle.

toast and orange juice — but it's all fresh and tasty.

The five girls who run it have to be keen to be in early each day to warm up the toaster and prepare the kettle.

Customer Jimmy Cartledge said the word had soon spread around school about Shaheen's.

"I come every day. I'd get nothing to eat in the morning without it," he said.

Fifteen-year-old Laura Hunt agreed. "It's worth coming in a bit earlier. The place has really caught on."

But headteacher Chris Searle revealed there was a serious side to the venture too.

"Shaheen's was set up with the help of a £900 grant from an initiative set up by the education authority to

promote better attendance and timekeeping," he said.

"It paid for the toaster and kettle and also the benches for the kids to sit on. At the moment everything for the students is free but the aim is to get it self-supporting."

The cafe was working well and was getting staff and students together in a friendly atmosphere before school.

"It gives us all a good start to the day and it is encouraging students to get here earlier," said Mr Searle.

■ Pictured at the pre-school cafe at Earl Marshal School are (left-right) Shaheen Akhtar, Dill Afroz, Naseen Jan, Basra Bi Bi and Naveed Khan

133

In a story on the cafe in the Sheffield *Star*, one of its protagonists, Afroz, declared: 'A lot of people don't get any breakfast at home, so there's been plenty of demand.' The girls managed to obtain a special grant from the LEA to pay for the toaster, kettle, crockery, milk, toast, orange juice, tea and cereal and the cafe soon became an important preschool social hub. And as the *Star* told it's readers through cafe regular Jimmy Cartledge: 'The word has soon spread around. I come every day. I'd get nothing to eat in the morning without it,' he said. And it also promoted better timekeeping and attendance too.

And these girls were tough. Every year we would organise fundraising school walks all around the Ladybower reservoirs in Derbyshire. We would take the entire school body for a day in coach-loads and walk a sponsored walk on the footpaths all around the huge man-made lakes and castle-like towers of dams where the 617 'Dam Busters' Squadron rehearsed their May 1943 attack on the Ruhr Valley dams with their Lancaster bombers and bouncing bombs over the serene high peaks and these very same reservoirs. Hundreds of our students would walk miles around the Howden and Derwent reservoirs and dams with our girls wearing their shalwar kameezes, and only the slightest, thinnest of footwear, almost barefoot, laughing and joking all the way round. How vibrant and full of life they were, girls in years but powerful women already in their minds, empathy and tenacity.

In mid-1994 some potentially dangerous divisions had broken out at school which teachers were finding it increasingly difficult to resolve. Arguments, leading to hostilities and the threat of dangerous behaviour had developed between groups of Pakistani and Somali boys. After-school encounters at local bus-stops and along the streets neighbouring the school had become menacing and sometimes insoluble. While talking about these problems with a group of senior Yemeni boys, one of them turned to me and said: 'Don't worry sir, we'll sort it out.' I knew how dedicated many of the community-active Yemeni boys were to peace and the withering away of division. Their own mother nation had been through hard and divisive years, was now a united country and many Sheffield Yemenis clearly wanted to keep it as such. They put enormous value on the qualities of unity, and this had passed on to their children – now, after years of separation of the two Yemens, they were English, and dedicated Sheffielders certainly, but also the proud supporters of a single, united Yemen. So the prospect of their school racked by internal division of two of its constituent communities was a future they would neither tolerate nor accept. They arranged a meeting between themselves and key representatives of the Pakistani and Somali boys. I told them to meet in my office. All afternoon, sitting outside the office, I could hear voices inside, sometimes angry, other times quieter and more apparently rational, sometimes laughing, sometimes in Arabic or Somali, but mostly in a shared Sheffield English. After two hours they emerged, smiling, with some back-slapping and embraces. 'We've sorted it! It'll be all reet now!' said one of the Yemeni boys. And it was too. The threatening ambiance dispersed and the altercations stopped. The students had done it by themselves, through their own minds and actions. They didn't need teachers. I couldn't have been more proud of them, and it was the incident that provoked the introduction of the 'Certificate of Peacemaking' presented in assemblies to those 'who have shown the eternal qualities of friendship and making peace with others, the hallmark of a true and

Earl Marshal School
Sheffield

Certificate of Peacemaking

This is to certify that

....

has shown the eternal qualities of friendship and making peace with others, the hallmark of a true and generous human being.

"The cause of peace is the hope of the world"

135

generous human being. The cause of peace is the hope of the world.' These were the words printed on the certificates below the image of the three doves flying from an open book.

One last example. In 1994 the Conservative government's Asylum Bill threatened dire consequences for refugees who had been refused British citizenship. They would be losing all benefits, including free school meals while they waited for their appeals to be heard. Senior students organised a co-educational protest involving boys and girls, in the form of a fashion parade – something not normally associated with progressive causes. Wearing sharp

new clothes and carrying a banner declaring 'Resist the racist Asylum Law,' they paraded along their own catwalk and posed for a telling, handsome photograph in the *Star*: Point exposed, point made, all by themselves. And one of the subjects in the photograph, Abtisam from the Yemeni community, twenty-five years later is a local Labour councillor and now a qualified solicitor and also holds the Sheffield Council cabinet responsibility for education and skills.

None of this 'actional' education was conceived as an alternative to the desk-inspired study and the vital need to master the established school curriculum: it was however an urgent and necessary supplement adding a fresh and crucial stimulation and motivation to bring real life to the examination-based curriculum, and critically sublimate its purposes. In fact, the school began to improve its GCSE results in 1991 and 1992, but with more second-language learners arriving in subsequent years, these examination advances began to fall away, provoking much institutional self-criticism and the quest for more successful ways to learn. Certainly I have never seen one approach counter-productive to the other, and I saw their integration exemplified time and time again at Earl Marshal.

But I had another fundamental educational belief that had always been a part of my learning and teaching: the principle of late development. My own education had certainly been generated through this: I was a secondary moderner who had failed crucial examinations at eleven years of age, and I needed more time, concentration and stimulus to educationally, cognitively and linguistically develop than many of my same-age contemporaries. At Earl Marshal I was teaching large numbers of teenagers in their second language who were frequently more attuned to other languages than English and who needed both more time and confidence to develop their English, even though their grasp of creative and poetical English was profound and often beautifully figurative. Yet they needed more linguistic knowledge, understanding and familiarity to develop all aspects of the language.

I often meet ex-students who, when they were at school, were struggling with limited English but who now are truly fluent and flourishing in the language. They have told me during ensuing years that they needed those early years of learning and unpressured consolidation in their second language before they could use it with the organic linguistic confidence that came later and which they now have in abundance. Since leaving school many of these ex-students have progressed to local colleges and as students of the two universities in the city as young and mature adults, gained degrees, but remain mindful that at Earl Marshal was where they learned their grounding English and language confidence upon which their later education was built. Their academic development came later, a truth that OFSTED have never and could never truthfully acknowledge, so preoccupied are they about instant examination success at sixteen, rather than a developmental success as achieved by our students in their later years.

Certainly the energy and consciousness of these young people was a powerful driving force for their education. The early 1990s was a very serious era for South Yorkshire pit communities close to Sheffield, and many of our students had close links to them. The National Union of Mineworkers was struggling to oppose the closure of pits, and we welcomed one of their officials, Terry Adair, to the school to speak to an assembly about the effect of the closures. Since our school had mounted its successful

1992 Earl Marshal students protest against pit closures.
photo: Martin Jenkinson.

campaign against closure, our students could feel a strong sense of empathy for miners and their communities. I was quoted in the Sheffield *Star*, as saying: 'As a school we share the sense of outrage when we hear that pits – which like schools are the centre of their communities – are to close. This is a vital educational issue. The whole country is discussing it, so schools should be doing so too.' Adair told the students: 'The closure programme can be seen as an attack on all working class families. For every miner's job lost there are two or three outside the pit to be lost. At the end of the day it's these pupils' job prospects that are being eroded too.' Fourth former Tricia Clayton needed no further impetus. She immediately set about writing a letter to Tory Prime Minister John Major. 'Have you thought about the implications of the jobs that will be lost?' she asked him. 'And have you thought about the fathers whose families are going to cope with no money? Already the children are asking their parents, 'What's for Christmas?' Most parents have to say "Sorry love, but your father is getting put out of his job because Mr Major is closing down the mines." Please keep the mines open for the children's sake!'

She never got a reply.

***

In 1993 one of my most creative and keenest students, a fifteen-year-old boy called Izat Khan, died through a chronic heart condition. Izat loved cricket and he loved writing poetry too, and was bold in defence of his own first and second languages – Panjabi and Urdu – as well as fully articulate and audacious in his third, English. He wrote a powerful assertion of his native language which was published in our anthology, *Valley of Words*:

Language

Speak the language you were born with,
Show your feelings to the people around you.
Show the people you are proud of your language,

139

Language is a great thing.
With language you can make friends.
People will know you as long as you live,
Language can help you to understand things around you,
Language can make you proud and happy,
Language will lead you to happiness.
Don't let anyone make fun of your language
Shout your language out to the people around you!
Let them know that you love your language
And you will speak your language as long as you live.
So shout your language out!

A group of students in their Needlework classes made a beautiful banner with a portrait of Izat in its centre and featuring his inspiring line: *Show the people you are proud of your language.* It was a moving tribute to a poet, a cricketer, a classmate and a lover of words, and it carried an elemental human power. Izat was in my GCSE English class, and every day he was a pleasure and a revelation to teach. I could only feel that I had lost a friend and wrote these words in his memory:

Poem for Izat:

Boy in a classroom
Class in a school
School in a community
Language our tool

City needs be of friendship
A valley of words
Flying between us
Words free as birds

Izat writing poems
Izat our brother
Listening to the voice
Of language, our mother

Izat in all of us
Smiling with his heart
Stretching his ambitions
Learning his part

His words are inside us
Keeping us alive
'Be proud of your language'
Making us thrive

Now shine the skies
In far Pakistan
And in the England of our eyes
The tears quietly ran

Life was his friend
His flesh and his brain
A voice that knows no end
That speaks every name

Your friends are beside you
Humans together
Learning the world
One blood that is forever

Chapter 5
Safa's Message

Looking back over three decades to the five and a half years of my time at Earl Marshal, I am lucky to be able to read the often astonishing poems, stories, and true-life experiences that were published in the four anthologies of that half-decade between 1990 and 1995: *Valley of Words, Lives of Love and Hope, School of the World* and *Heart of Sheffield.* The books are supplemented in my memory by visits from some remarkable writers. John Agard we have already met, and in his introduction to *School of the World,* he wrote about the qualities of imaginative empathy the writers expressed and told them: 'Your identification with Quddus in his state of coma is a touching demonstration of giving voice to the pain of someone brutally reduced to a voiceless state. In your journey pieces, you share the freshness of your impressions of places most of us will never see in our lifetime: Mecca, Brunei, Curacao, Kashmir, Benin, Aden.' He concluded that in their writings 'we begin to sense something of the deep need for utterance which connects human beings across the planet.'

Powerful words from a Guyanese and universal heart. Another such heart was that of the South African novelist Mandla Langa, who visited the school in 1992 and wrote the introduction to *Valley of Words,* at the same time that his nation was freeing itself from apartheid after a marathon struggle. The students had written many

Mandla Langa.

143

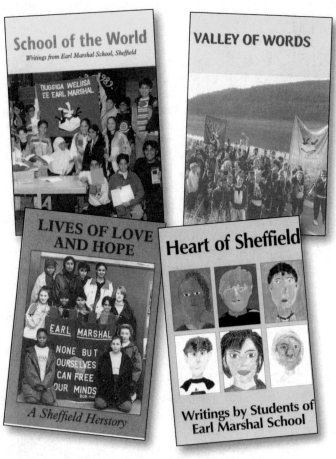

The four anthologies printed between 1990 and 1995:

poems imagining the torment of those in the heart of that struggle. Langa's identification with the young Sheffield writers was total, as their words had been with him and his people. 'As South Africans in the ANC,' he wrote, 'we are proud to be associated with these young poets. We are also moved by their understanding of the struggle and what it entails. The writers' priorities and concerns left me with hope that the future will be full of young people who will refuse to be part of a society whose main preoccupation is wealth and prestige. All power to their pens.' If you read Langa's classic novel,*Tenderness of Blood,* and then read our young poets' words, you are exploring the very same soul. In her poem, *Hector's Story,* Shameem wrote about Hector Pietersen, the first child shot down at the massacre of Soweto in July 1976. Her lines are lucid and direct; any true poet would want to create them, for in their brevity is sheer power.

As he marched
Freedom on his lips,
Hands in the air,
Screaming, shouting,
'Africa is mine!'
Suddenly,
Soldiers shout
You fell, I ran,
You bled, I cry,
You died, I lived
My son, a martyr.

Or there is Naeeda's poem, bringing together a word she knows with the same word which means a different world of pain in South Africa.

In Detention

I'm in detention
For not doing my homework.

They're in detention
For crying for freedom.
I'll be home in two hours
They'll be home in two months
Or maybe more.

They might not even come back.
They'll be tortured,
I won't.
They'll be hanged like clothing
I won't.

How many lives
Will be lost?
How many mothers will shed tears?
How many loved ones will die,
Die before Africa gets its freedom?

South Africa had just won its freedom after decades of struggle against Apartheid, but for the Palestinians, the struggle went on against another apartheid and the power of our students' imaginative empathy enabled them to begin to understand it and express it in the classroom. Sajid used his words to express the anguish of a Palestinian woman waiting for her combatant husband to return.

Love in Palestine

Now you go to fight,
How do I know if you will return?
You have gone now,
The time has passed and you're not back.
Oh my love, your children cry!
I hope you will be here to see them live.
For a year now I have been waiting
For you to walk through that door!

And Faheem remembered the Nablus martyr Ayman Jamous, killed by his occupiers while resisting in the Intifada:

Intifada

Why does it have to be this way,
Bullying at night and fighting all day?
I throw stones and rocks with my own brave hands,
Remembering my brother who lay dead in the sands,
Shot by the army and the police -
We don't want war, we want peace!
Why does it have to be like this,
Losing your family without a blessing or a kiss?
I'm losing a part of my life every day,
Why can't we just throw war away?

146

I walk the streets in fear of a soldier,
My fist closed and within it a boulder.
We all fight as one under the sun,
Yet this war has not been won.
We throw stones, they pull the trigger,
What falls to the ground is a tall dark figure,
'Ayman Jamous! Ayman Jamous!'
Why can't we call this war to a truce?

Nadia expressed a deep and abiding love for a stolen country.

Life Land

It was a normal day
A normal morning
And a normal unhappy feeling.

I went to a market
To buy all I can afford
For my family.
When a man dressed in a green suit
A cap, and carrying a rifle
(And that made him a soldier
And that gave him the right to order me around)
Suddenly stopped me with his rifle.
He pointed it at me,
Asking me where is my identity card.
Identity? We are the Palestinians!
We were born free
In our father's and grandfather's land called Palestine –
The Holy Land.
We have our identity
Not just in Palestine but throughout the whole world,
And it destroys the happiness and joy in our hearts
And it destroys our children too!
The children
Children who don't have freedom anymore
They don't have the freedom to enjoy
They don't have a future to finish their education.
They want to build their future
But deep, deep inside
They know the Israelis won't give them a chance.
It is all right for Israeli children,

147

They have the right
Yes, they have the right to be free
And to have a bright future -
Because they have a life-land
A land not taken over by other people.
Our children
As soon as they learn to walk
They need to learn to carry a weapon!
They have to
Our children!

They would love to go to school
And to hold a pen and pencil like
Other children around the world.
After all, we are all the same
But nobody, nobody will give them a chance.

And we cry
Cry for all the world
Cry for the Israeli government
To give us our freedom and our country.
You know the Israeli system -
Why, why do they treat us like this?

Democracy, democracy, just for Israelis -
Palestinians are not included.
In the name of Allah,
We don't ask much from the Israeli government,
But just for all the Palestinians
To be free and live like everybody else in this world,
To be with our families
To sleep in our homes in peace
And to hope for a glorious morning!

Many of these poems were read in morning assemblies. I
remember one when Musa, a Somali lad who was often in
and out of trouble, read out a long passage imagining
himself as a stone-throwing boy during the Intifada, telling
his story. Musa's audience was gripped as they had never
seen him in this light before. Here is one of his paragraphs,
written the day before in his English class one morning in
1992. In its depth and empathy it still carries the truth of
now-times.

We throw stones, they pull the trigger. What is their hobby, Murder? Or is it the enjoyment of seeing us suffer with pain and sorrow? When we throw, they get grazed. When they shoot, we die. How can they sleep knowing they killed someone's loved one? Old women, men, children, and babies? They will not rest until they've wiped us out. In the West people have freedom and love, but the Israelis do not know the word *love* nor loyalty. All they know is murder and violence. America can help us by stopping their supply of weapons. But to them money is more precious than life.

We had many fine writers visit the school and talk to and inspire the young writers. The Jamaican novelist Joan Riley, author of *The Unbelonging* and *Waiting in the Twilight* taught a session to a large group of senior girls, telling them that she was a working-class girl like they were, and that it was hard work and believing in herself that made her into a professional writer. Barry Hines, the Yorkshire novelist of *A Kestrel for a Knave* and the Sheffield-based *Looks and Smiles* which we were studying at the time, came into one of my English classes and

Joan Riley's seminar.

Musa's assembly.

gave my students a similar message. The Pakistani
novelist Rukhsana Ahmad was impressed by the 'unex-
pected richness' of the students' writing. And not only

Rukhsana Ahmad's seminar, Earl Marshal, 1993.

writers came. The veteran comic actor Bill Owen, who for years had played the mischievous Compo in *Last of the Summer Wine* and before that had been a stalwart alongside Paul Robeson at the Unity Theatre, and had written a musical about the Bow Matchgirls, spent a day at the school, and in June 1992 he named school's theatre and assembly hall The Bill Owen Theatre. He told the Sheffield *Star*: 'I have been in entertainment for 57 years and this is the greatest honour I have ever received.' The students milled around him, joking and laughing, loving his humour. My old friend Trevor Huddleston, ex-Bishop of Stepney, ex-Archbishop of the Indian Ocean in Mauritius and veteran anti-apartheid campaigner travelled up from London and spoke about his return to South Africa after Apartheid's end, and the young writer and anti-racist activist Liz Fekete from the Institute of Race Relations, spent an afternoon with a group of senior

Bill Owen at Earl Marshal.
photo: Sheffield Newspapers Ltd.

ANTI-Apartheid leader Bishop Trevor Huddleston urged city pupils to press for equality in South Africa.

The worldwide president of the Anti-Apartheid Association revealed to students at Earl Marshal School his own experiences in South Africa and explained the present political situation.

He said: "There is a great deal of misunderstanding

By Fiona Firth

about at the moment. People think that Apartheid is over, but it's not.

"The next six months are going to be decisive. South Africa is moving towards a new constitution and democratic elections for all races.

"But if a negotiated settlement can't be reached, the whole African continent could explode."

He added: "It is up to us to put massive pressure on our government and western Europe to make sure Apartheid is abolished."

A group of Somali pupils also told of their experiences escaping war and famine in their country.

Fir Vale head Chris Searle said: "It was a very deep and moving experience for pupils to meet a person of such stature."

Pupils urged to fight for equality

Trevor Huddleston's visit.

students talking about her work – and their work and writing too. Earl Marshal became a hub of writers, performers and activists. The Cuban youth leader Pavel Diaz Hernandez spoke about the effect of the US blockade on his country, and on two separate occasions, first Sunduza – the Zimbabwean dance group performed and scooped up dozens of students in traditional and contemporary dancing, while a few weeks later the Nigerian dancers of the Port Harcourt Dance Company showed their enormous physical and musical virtuosity. It was all part of an international curriculum for an internationalist school and its community. The reviewer of *School of the World* in the *Yorkshire Post* – not renowned for its progressive editorial views, began his uncharacteristic piece by stating the names of the Home Secretary and Foreign Secretary in the Conservative government in power in 1994:

> Forget Michael Howard and Douglas Hurd. Forget the United Nations. Throw them all on the scrap heap and fill up the vacancies with appointees from Sheffield's School of the World.
>
> The pupils of Earl Marshal Comprehensive in Fir Vale, on the edge of the old steel-making heartland, have just published their third anthology of poems and prose with a strong anti-racist and internationalist theme.
>
> Contributions from among the 600 students include pieces on racist attacks and bullying. Shameem Hussain tells the story in poetry of how she was attacked by five white boys who'd picked on her because she'd bought a white dress to celebrate the Moslem festival of Eid. They said it was the wrong colour for a black girl. Some of the experiences described by the writers whose school is 85% black should make a white reader hang their head in shame.
>
> But the overriding impression is that of a group of young people who rejoice inside their own skin and in being part of a rich multicultural community. They long for peace – in their own lives and in the world.

I don't think I've ever read anything like this, before or since, in the *Yorkshire Post*. As for Shameem's poem, here it is:

Black Dresses

Eid was coming up
I was excited to go to Meadowhall
To buy myself a long dress.
I saw a white dress,
It had embroidery at the top and bottom,
Small black flowers inside.
It was nice, so I bought it for £10.
As I left the shop
Five white boys came out of the arcades.
They pushed me about
As if I'm not a human being
But some kind of dirt.
They snatched the dress off me

153

They told me white wasn't the right colour
So they put the dress in the mud
They swung it over my head
Then handed it over to me.
The dress was all ruined,
I cried, it hurt in my heart.
One of the boys told me to 'look there!'
I looked into the shop
There were plain long black dresses.
They told me to wear those on Eid.
I left the muddy dress
I wiped my tears
I walked along the empty streets
And came home in the darkness.

***

I first met Devon Malcolm in the mid-80s, when he was a young cricketer breaking through into county cricket and playing for Derbyshire. He wasn't allowed to play for Yorkshire, even though his family home was in Wincobank, Sheffield, because he had been born in his parents' birthplace, Jamaica. I went with him and Mike Atkins to visit the Haringey Cricket College in north London, set up to

Steve Taylor, Devon Malcolm, Chris Searle and Mike Atkins, 1993.

154

'Devon Malcolm's Cricket Centre's young cricketer

bring on black and working-class young cricketers into the county game. We were very impressed by its success and the commitment of its organisers, and we resolved to set up something with similar objectives in Sheffield.

When I was appointed to Earl Marshal we had a ripe opportunity to pursue this dream. There was a school population, particularly among the Pakistani boys, who loved cricket – the Imran Khan visit had demonstrated that right across the school's catchment area – and a large sports hall with cricket nets. We also had a CDT teacher, Owen Gittens, like Mike from Barbados, who was a longstanding organiser and player of Sheffield Caribbean Cricket Club who as a young man had served in the RAF in Aden, so he had much to discuss with the Yemeni students. There was also a potential teaching assistant in Steve Taylor, who like Devon was a very quick bowler who had played for Derbyshire Second XI, and was also deeply involved with Sheffield Caribbean. So Steve came onto our staff. He lived in Pitsmoor and many of our students knew him already, so he became a precious community asset as well as a superb coach. There weren't many urban comprehensive schools who employed a cricket coach (although Steve had many mainstream Physical Education tasks too); that was much more a feature of the elite public schools, but for us, cricket had a very different motivating function. As the promising fifteen-year-old Tahir put it: 'Cricket has built up my courage never to lose hope and to teach us there is always a chance.'

This was put with insight and understanding in a May 1995 article in *The Observer* by the Australian sports journalist Kevin Mitchell, who spent a day at the school. This is a part of what he wrote in his article, *Mean Streets Feel the Pace of Change*:

There is a special feel about Sheffield, tucked away in the rough, rolling hills of South Yorkshire. What others say they can't do, they invariably do, stubbornness informed by a history of struggle, steel running through their past in fact and inclination.

It is palpable at Earl Marshal School in the north of the city. Here in the blighted district of Fir Vale, where mass unemployment and crime give even a sunny day a hard edge, smiling brown faces, sons of the huge immigrant community, draw comfort from the simple pleasure of bat and ball.

The headteacher is Chris Searle, an Essex man and cricket lover who brings a tireless zeal to his work. He is quietly proud of his charges and proud too of the inspiration behind a rare and exciting venture, the Devon Malcolm Cricket Centre. It is heartwarming on a grand scale and Searle's politics of care drives his enthusiasm. He points to Wincobank Hill, a mound of earth with symbolism entwined in every blade of grass. It was here that the Romans found the locals unmovable for an irritatingly long time, tucked up in their Celtic fort. It was not far from here, either, that the Chartists blossomed. It was here that the city of steel lingered in the old trade longer than many expected in the face of recession. It was here where the miners drew much comfort during their year-long strike.

'This is not just about cricket,' Searle says. 'It is about responding to cultural strength in the community. And

Devon Malcolm, 1994, with his bowling machine gift.

around here it is a culture of resistance. What these kids learn through cricket, they can take back into their studies. I'm a great believer in team games and cricket stimulates unity and provides collective solutions to problems. In that regard, Devon, who is a powerful cricketer, probably the fastest bowler in the world, has been exceptional. He is a genuine and committed human being. C.L.R. James said the most important thing about the game is that a cricketer should be returned to the community. Devon exemplifies that. He has never left his roots and is a great example for other cricketers.'

'The real strength of British cricket lies in the inner cities, which the game's administrators have never realised. There are players in these cities who can form the nucleus of a world-beating England team, particularly among the arrivant communities, but they are simply not being developed.'

I would be asked time and time again why so much energy and attention was put on cricket at our school. Some advisers, OFSTED inspectors and education officers would scoff and laugh at our cricket centre. Yet the participation was

157

huge – every lunchtime the sports hall and nets would be full of young cricketers – the Yemenis, Somalis were there too, and some of the girls too were increasingly getting involved. Mandela's words resonated with me: 'Sport has the power to change the world, the power to inspire, the power to unite people in a way that little else can. It also speaks to people in a language they understand.' As Tahir put it in poetry:

When I bat and bowl
I remember the courage I had lost
And what cricket had brought back.

When Devon took his 9–57 and bowled out the still predominantly white South Africa team at the Oval in 1994, there was genuine excitement within the school, particularly when Devon gave a detailed talk about his achievement in the school's resources area, and showed a video of his bowling feat, commenting upon each wicket that fell. He visited the school regularly, donated a bowling machine that could hurl down the ball even faster than he could, and his winnings from the case in 1995 against the establishment *Wisden Cricket Monthly,* which had published an article stating that Black players playing for England 'feel satisfaction, perhaps subconsciously, at seeing England humiliated' – were given half to the cricket centre at Earl Marshal and half to the Derbyshire Children's Hospital which cared for his daughter Natalie when she was seriously ill. The *Caribbean Times* was elated at Devon's victory off the cricket field, headlining their article *Sweet Dreams are made of this!* They went on to report:

Chris Searle, headmaster of the Earl Marshal School where the centre is based, said: 'This is typical of Devon. He is dedicated to the community where he first played his cricket. It is just fantastic that he has made cricket pay up for its racism. He is a wonderful example for all the youngsters we have here.'

The school children at the centre have their own battle to face against cricket's established racist attitudes. Based in the heart of South Yorkshire, the youngsters of Pakistani, Yemeni and African-Caribbean background know all too well that the County Cricket Club have never had a black native of Yorkshire on their staff.

How heartwarming that money from *Wisden Cricket Monthly*, the guardian of conservatism in cricket, will now help them to realise their dream!

As CLR James had put it in *Beyond the Boundary,* so succinctly, so wisely: 'What do they know of cricket, that only cricket know?' When Devon toured South Africa in 1995 and met Mandela in Soweto, the President of South Africa said to him, 'I know you, you are the destroyer!' And he was from our community, from the heart of Sheffield. As he wrote in his autobiography *You Guys are History!* in 1998:

The idea is to help them develop cricket skills and with Chris Searle there as the inspirational driving force, the kids can learn so much. Chris is a former headteacher and is the founder of the centre. He's done a fantastic unifying job. With such a racial mix at the Centre, there's genuine hope that the youngsters will grow up to respect not just their own culture but others as well. I remember playing for Asian sides in Sheffield, and I enjoyed getting to know about their religion, how they lived their lives. Cricket teaches you respect for others. Sheffield Caribbean Club, where I first learned about cricket in any depth after coming over from Jamaica, was so important for me at a time of my life when I might have drifted, just like many other black kids. They put in so much hard work on my behalf, encouraging me to bowl fast and even organising transport for me. I still keep in touch with them and I'll always be grateful to them. So the Devon Malcolm Centre is my attempt to bind young people in the community.

Devon's message was reinforced in January 1994 by another great cricketer when Gordon Greenidge, the Barbados-born West Indies opening batsman spoke at an assembly at Earl Marshal. But he didn't just talk about cricket, he emphasised the necessity of buckling down to serious learning, saying how much an influence on his early years John Arlott, the great cricket commentator, like

Greenidge a Hampshire man, had been. He was 'the Shakespeare of cricket,' declared Greenidge, 'and made me understand how language and self-expression are so important to young lives.' The students listened intently: the Bill Owen Theatre was alive with concentration as he spoke. So speaking, writing and the development of brain power went hand in glove with hitting and square-cutting a ball as brilliantly as the great Greenidge. It was an early morning lesson well-taken and well-remembered.

A couple of years ago I met up with Devon again after two and a half decades. I found myself playing for a team of Caribbean veterans, including Devon, in an end-of-season match against the regular Sheffield Caribbean team at their ground in Ecclesfield in the north of the city. As I arrived with Mike, I found him still strong and fit, discussing with some of the regular players how he could donate a new sight-screen for the ground from his cricket equipment company. He hadn't changed in either his generosity and commitment to the local club that had bred and provided for him when he was a teenager.

Batting with him I saw up close the huge force with which he still hit the ball as it disappeared over the long-on boundary out of the ground. When he was out, Sam Gittens, like Mike another Barbadian stalwart, came in to bat. I was 74, Sam was 78, so we had 152 between us before we'd even scored a run. Running up and down the wicket like a couple of crazed teenagers, my whole life came sweeping back. At the end of the match and in the pavilion over jerk chicken and Red Stripe Jamaican beer, I was proud to make a speech about Devon's achievement, both as a cricketer and demolition man of exclusive white South African cricket, and in Earl Marshal as a true sportsman who never turned aside from those young people who came after him. And as I spoke I saw the faces of hundreds of young Sheffielders who had been inspired by him, and the sheer, rampant speed of his bowling.

It wasn't just cricket either. Earl Marshal students found a firm friend in the young Sheffield Wednesday footballer,

Chris Bart-Williams whose own Sierra Leone childhood touched a close empathy with their life-stories. He became a regular visitor to the school, relaxing with them, speaking at assemblies and taking an important role in the 'No More Hiroshimas' events organised at the school. We organised a five-a-side football competition, naming the teams after cities that had been savagely bombed in different wars. There were teams called Dresden, Coventry, Harg-

Chris Bart-Williams

eisa, Hiroshima, Hanoi, Grozny, Sarajevo and Guernica, and Chris volunteered to be referee of the matches. In a letter featured in the Sheffield *Star*, an enraged reader wrote to the paper, condemning his support of the world peace effort. I wrote back defending the young player and my letter took prominence as the 'Star Letter' of the day. I wrote:

> Chris Bart-Williams speaks for another generation whose minds and actions all over are set on peace. He is himself a living example of this.
>
> Far from being the mercenary and mindless footballer so wrongly portrayed in Mr Mooney's letter, Chris has shown tremendous social commitment and service to young people in Sheffield since he first came to play at Hillsborough.
>
> He has organised coaching sessions for school students (including Earl Marshal) and worked devotedly and imaginatively to secure a better future for young Sheffielders.
>
> As well as being an excellent on-the-field example as a self-disciplined, unselfish and creative footballer with brilliant footwork and passing skills, he is showing us how footballers are also thinking people who have a brain and vision beyond a football pitch.
>
> Every strength to you, Chris!

Remembering the victims

DON'T let history dictate the future — that's the message head teacher Chris Searle has been getting over to Earl Marshal pupils in the wake of VE Day and the run-up to anniversary of Hiroshima.

"We felt quite strongly about the anniversary of the dropping of the atom bomb because the Japanese have been left out of all these VE Day celebrations and we wanted to make sure they were not forgotten," said Chris.

Pupils have spent a month looking at the consequences of Hiroshima.

"They've watched slides and seen the consequences of what happens when you unleash an atomic weapon on people. typing of the Japanese, their art, poetry, and culture," said Chris.

Refugees

They also looked at other cities that have suffered through bombing in the last 50 years including Dresden, Coventry, Hanoi, and Hargeisa

in Somalia, the home of many of the school's pupils who were forced to flee the bombardment in 1990.

"You can't allow history to dictate the future. You mustn't become a prisoner of history because the peace process has to move ahead," said Chris.

"We finished up with an unusual six-a-side football match. refereed by Chris Bart-Williams from Sheffield Wednesday, with each team representing one of the bombed cities."

Certainly the 'No More Hiroshimas' football also had its impact in the classroom. It stimulated us to read extracts from John Hersey's classic account, *Hiroshima* and much creative writing and discussion came out of it, such as Ghamdan and Fiaz's collaboratively-written poem, *Mizu* (Japanese for 'water'):

'Mizu! Mizu!'
Say the people of Hiroshima,
'We want water!'
A man comes to help,
He jumps onto a sandpit
Of one of the rivers of Ota.
He looks around him
And hundreds of people are saying
'Mizu! Mizu!'
He says, 'there is no clean water,

The water is poisoned
And the only clean water runs down your face.
It is your tears.'

And as for the promised £14.95 Colibri Elgin ballpoint pen, the prize for the 'Star Letter,' it kept me going for a few months.

In 1994 our anthology, *Lives of Love and Hope* became runner-up in the national competition for the Raymond Williams Community Publishing Award. Ironically for me, the winner was a book from my old East London borough, Tower Hamlets, written by residents living in the radically changing cityscape of the Isle of Dogs. *Lives of Love and Hope* was a collection of biographical interviews of their mothers, aunts and grandmothers, done by the students often in their first languages, then translated, where necessary. I was helped in the classroom tasks by an old school friend, writer and university teacher, Lesley Holly. Moving life stories of women growing up in Pakistan, Pitsmoor, Somalia, Yemen, Grimesthorpe, Jamaica, Kashmir, Syria, Sylhet in Bangladesh and Fir Vale showed the intense internationalism and life-wisdom of our communities, all sparked by a startling thematic poem written by Emteaz, one of our teaching assistants, called *Born to Fight*:

I was born a daughter of a steel-worker
Son of a farmer from a land in the East
Full of colour, spices, warmth and smells
Pain and hunger, fear and oppression.

I was born a daughter of a steel-worker
Baby of a mother with the name Asha
Daughter of a farmer from a land in the East
And we were sown, watered, fed and grown.

And we struggled as we were moulded and formed in the heat
Because I was born a daughter of a steel-worker.

And I kicked and I ran to face the night
With those hungry and those desperate searching eyes

163

I faced reality
In the homeless and the shame of the rejected.

And I ran and danced to face the night
And from the lightness and darkness
There formed a balance
Because I was born the daughter of a steel-worker.

And we were raised in the life of love and hope
Because I was born a daughter of a steel-worker
And the baby of a mother with the name of Asha
And I was raised in the light and I was born to fight.

Of all the anthologies I have done of my students' work, this one must be the most intense, carrying the most bitter and exalting truth. In the story by Asma, called *Amala,* she begins by recalling her childhood village in Sylhet. It was as the complete contrary to Pitsmoor:

My name is Sofia Begum. I was born in Sylhet, a district in rural Bangladesh, in the north-east of the country. The village where I was born was a fine and beautiful place; it had nearly everything one could expect. The place was extremely clean, with no litter lying around. Most of the people who lived in the village cared about the place very much and did their best to keep it well and tidy. To me the people were environmentalists. When one came to the village, one could see and smell the green grass and also smell the perfume from the different types of flowers. There were also ponds which had clean, clear water, where one could see many diverse fishes, most of them were bright colours. The pond was extremely pretty with the water lilies and white pebbles down beneath the bottom, which appeared to look like pearls. Probably that was why the village was called Suna Pur (Village of Gold).

She tells the story of an oppressive marriage, migration to London, in Southall, and eventually to Sheffield. Suddenly, a cluster of sentences leaped at me from Asma's pages as the account took on an even more powerful salience:

There was one particular anti-racist demonstration in Southall – it's clear in my mind even though I wasn't there

164

at the time. A man named Blair Peach, a white anti-racist, was brutally killed by police after their intervention in the demonstration. Blair was described by many as a man full of love and care, who looked at people as one, instead of their colour. He was a man with a brave mind, who died fighting for us. Saleh had gone to the demonstration with friends from the local community. He said that when he had heard that Blair was killed everything appeared upside down. When I saw people crying because of his death, I knew how much this man, who abhorred racism, meant to them.

As I read this I could only marvel. Here I was in Sheffield a decade and a half after Blair's death and he was still with me in the classroom, and still with thousands of others too.

In her introduction to *Lives of Love and Hope,* Rukhsana Ahmad wrote: 'Despite the recognition by the young writers of the harshness of some of their mothers' experiences, the volume resonates with optimism and love rather than despair and self-pity.' She quotes from the narrative of Safa, born in Aden and a relative newcomer to the school whose brilliant young mind picked up English with an astonishing speed, and she was very soon writing poems and stories with a telling poetic lucidity in her second language. Her first poem in English was a praise song to her new city published in *Valley of Words,* called *The Future of Sheffield:*

This is the place I live in
The place I love.
Sheffield is my place
Sheffield is my country.
I came here and I don't know why
Maybe because I want to stay here
Or because I love it, or... or... or...
I don't know, but the thing I do know is
That I don't want to leave it.

It's a nice place for all people,
Its hands are always open for all people,
For every kind of people, every colour of people -
They're never closed, its hands, never... never...
We have to make it more beautiful.

165

When I went to visit her parents after she had been in school for a few months, I could tell them of the ripe progress she was making. I saw that her father was blind and I was told he was a Yemeni hero, with a street in Aden holding his name. Her story in *Lives of Love and Hope* told me why. She wrote that when her mother was a girl, 'Aden was very dangerous because of the British occupation, which had started in 1838. So the people of Aden suffered a lot.' Then she continued:

After two years of fighting the British army, the man who wanted to marry my mother got blinded when he was fighting with my grandfather against some British soldiers. They shot my father in his eyes. At that time he didn't want anything from his life because he had lost his sight. He thought that his life was finished. They brought a doctor for him but he couldn't do anything for my father. So he became a blind man at the age of sixteen.

So my mother got married to my father when she was just thirteen years old. She was very young to get married but she hadn't any choice. She was so young to understand the life of marriage. Being a woman, a woman who was going to share a life with a man who couldn't see anything at all, that time was the hardest time for both of them – for my mother and my father. She couldn't understand him because she was still very young and he couldn't understand himself either, becoming a blind person now for the rest of his life, living in the darkness all the time, not knowing what was going on around him. They shared some very hard, sad moments in their lives.

But she was a real woman because she was taking care of my father very much. She understood how he felt and she did her best to change him into a real man and a lucky man like he had been before, and better than before. At first he used to shout at her and beat her because she was the person who was with him all the time. For when you lose your eyes, what can you do without them? It was very hard for him and for her too. But the years went past and this woman was very lucky to change her husband to a person who can see with his heart, not just with his eyes.

When I read this I felt like a lucky man to have met, and through their daughter's interpretation skills, talked to them. I also marvelled at Safa's new brilliance with English. Soon after, I was asked to visit Yemen as a guest of the new, unified government. They looked after me like an honoured guest, with visits to the Ministry of Education in Sanaa and several schools. For me, the uncanny truth was that almost everyone that I met in Yemen had heard of Earl Marshal, and teachers and education officers were referring to it as colonies in the old British Empire used to talk about Eton or Harrow. It certainly wasn't anything like them but the Yemenis knew all about it and seemed to love its reputation. Perhaps it was that so many of their friends or relatives' children had been welcomed into the school almost as soon as they got off the plane, with no bureaucracy and the minimum of formality; perhaps it was because every Saturday and Sunday at their language school at Earl Marshal, it was full of Yemeni children learning Arabic or their country's history and geography; or perhaps it was because of students like fourteen-year-old Safa, who learned English with so much speed and eloquence, and who had written her special poem for International Women's Day:

Your Day, Woman!

This is your day, woman
All over the world!
I'm very happy
That they made a special
Day for you.
    It doesn't matter
If I'm a man or woman,
But it does matter
If we don't know what it means
For all the people in the world.
    Woman made man.
She always works in everything.
She is the mother and she is the doctor.
She is the cure for everything,
So we must do everything for the woman.

167

I'll just try to do something for her
Maybe it will only be a quarter of what she deserves,
By writing this small poem for her.

In late 1994 the school applied to join the Federation of
Worker Writers and Community Publishers, the first school
ever to do so. In an article in their quarterly journal,
FEDeration, Nick Pollard describes the visit to the school
that he and two colleagues made, and the assembly they
were invited to, with students reading their work from
School of the World. The poem by Khadeegha, from Syria,
particularly moved him. He wrote: 'Certainly this collection
has an international focus, mostly on racism and political
freedom, whether it be in Sheffield's Meadowhall, Low Edges
and Attercliffe, Palestine, South Africa and Yemen. Hardly a
corner of the world is untouched; not even *The Undiscovered
Land.*' He quoted the extraordinary poem in full and added:
'This is resounding poetry, with a thumping challenge at the
end. We remarked on the issues that the writers have chosen
when many people writing poetry think it should all be about
hearts and flowers.' Khadeegha's words had a very different
trajectory, one that is as yet unknown and the land of future
generations but what we know is that she eventually gained
a doctorate in Education, and became a university professor
in Abu Dhabi.

The Undiscovered Land

Our language is unwritten,
Our history is untold,
Our deeds are passed down from father to son,

You constructed a path for my enemy,
you broke your promise.

The shedding of our agony,
caused frozen tears to appear on the faces of the unfor-
given.

Our land was the land of beauty,
the land of dreams,

the land of happiness,
the land of harmony,
For it was the land of nature.

The golden shafts of sunlight,
beaming through the mountain maze,
at emerald stalks of young flowers,
blossoming in golden corn fields.

The evening clouds,
hovering pink in the fading light,
above distant snow peaks;
the land of beauty.

The only path that leads to our undiscovered land,
is through the caves of destiny.
    You will never live to foretell our history
For this is the undiscoverable land.

At the close of my last Summer term at Earl Marshal, a
young Asian colleague and I took a group of twenty or so
senior students for a week to London. We stayed at the
youth hostel in the shadow of St. Paul's and met local MP
Richard Caborn, who took us into the House of Commons,
where we watched proceedings from the Public Gallery.
Most of the students seemed bemused and disinterested
and kept looking at me to see if it was time to go. But the
day that really grasped them was when we went to East
London. We spent some time walking around Whitechapel
and Spitalfields, and they were fascinated by the Bengali
street life, the sweatshops, restaurants and the Fournier
Street mosque that had once been a church, then a syna-
gogue and now a mosque, and the houses that had
sheltered Huguenots, Irish, Jews and Bangladeshis. They
remembered well what had happened to Quddus and his
friends in these very same streets just a year or so before.
For me, it was going back a quarter of a century to the same
streets where many of my former students had lived, also
there was Princelet Street, a tributary of Brick Lane, the
birthplace of *Stepney Words*. It was a strange amalgam:
Spitalfields and Pitsmoor. In 1970, a thirteen-year-old boy

called Tony had written these lines in his poem, *Brick Lane*, the street where he lived:

> Brick Lane is a horrible place
> Where everyone has a gloomy face,
> There isn't one little space to play football.
> Everyone plays in the dirt
> Filling all their hair with dirt
> What a place.
> I always try to be happy and cheerful,
> Now I begin to get doubtful.

Now, in 1994, Zulfiqar from Pitsmoor, Sheffield, also wrote a poem with the same title:

> Brick Lane, a lane of pain for some.
> Brick Lane, a lane of destruction for some.
> The West End is a treat for some,
> The East End is a beast for some.
> While the West End makes money
> The East End goes broke.
> I walked through the West End
> I walked through the East End,
> I saw differences.
> The money in one place
> The poverty in the other,
> The tall buildings in one
> Small crumbling buildings in the other.
> Brick Lane, so quiet that morning
> As if the Black Death had returned.
> But with the racism of the BNP
> This time it has changed its colour to white.

And Farooq's poem could have come from the pages of *Our City*, of a decade earlier, so close and bonded to the London streets as it was:

> As I went through the light of London,
> The West End of London,
> I began thinking what a good place London is!
> The buildings like huge mountains,
> The crowds of people,
> The riches in the atmosphere -

All the surroundings were caught in my eyes.

The next day I went to the East of London.
As I saw the life around me
I didn't know if the place was London or not.
Most of the shops were barred up
To stop racists breaking the windows.
There was broken glass
From the shop windows.
There were mainly Asians around.
Then when I went past a notice board, it said:
'Don't vote for the BNP'.
As I read it, then I knew
Racism had captured life there.
This street was called Brick Lane -
Near the place where Quddus Ali was attacked
Where Jack the Ripper killed the women.
The East gave me a different view
From what I saw in the West End of London.

The one thing I will always remember
Is that although London may be a good city,
And it might have Britain's most famous places.
And might be the richest place in Britain,
It's also the poorest.
It might be full of life,
But it's also full of death.

He had discovered another city full of contrasts – like his
own, two hundred miles north, but a capital city where the
gulf in class and wealth seemed even more startling.

As we waited for the coach back to Yorkshire at Victoria
Coach Station, many of the students seemed disturbed by
surprise at the extremes they had seen in London. Some
had not been before, others had been filled with images of
pomp, royalty and privilege before they went. But as they
told me on the coach home, the truth often startles as well
as hurts.

Chapter 6
Excluded Again!

My first encounter with a British school governing body had been neither a constructive or harmonious one, and resulted in my sacking in May 1971 from Sir John Cass and Redcoat School in Stepney, East London. My campaign for reinstatement, supported by a student strike, the National Union of Teachers and the Inner London Education Authority, resulted in my return to the school in May 1973. But my relationship with governors of Earl Marshal school was an entirely different reality. The all-male, all-white governing body of Sir John Cass had mainly been made up of Church of England clerics and City businessmen: the Earl Marshal governors by 1994 held a majority of representatives of Sheffield's black communities, and several highly experienced educational professionals. There was a Pakistani taxi driver and a Pakistani steelworker, who lived very close to the school campus and kept a close watching brief over it; a veteran Pakistani youth worker, a man held in high respect for his decades of committed work. He called the school the community's 'second home.' Abdul Shaif, Chair of the Yemeni Community Association who was also a SUMES coordinator of Community Liaison was vice-chair to chair Mike Atkins who was still Director of the City Council's Race Equality Unit and very active in SADACCA. Mrs Sheel was a middle-aged and experienced member of the Somali Community Association. In addition, there was a headteacher of a special school for so-called 'maladjusted' pupils with everyday involvement in teaching children excluded from mainstream schools and the Deputy Head of an inner-city primary school. Two elected teacher-governors were also crucial members. No other school in Sheffield had a comparable governance: Earl Marshal was the first and only Sheffield school, before or since, to have black majority membership.

Earl Marshal under its previous leadership was one of the schools that the Exclusions Survey of 1986 had shown to have had a disproportionate amount of black exclusions. So this governing body was determined to deal seriously and radically with exclusion *per se*, as by 1995 80% of Earl Marshal's 550 pupils were from Sheffield's black communities. Also, the number of black staff had grown from four in 1990 to twenty-one in 1995, so there was a general awareness amongst governors and many of the teachers that exclusion was a negative and destructive dimension of school life, was integral to past structures of institutional racism, and should be rejected as an accepted disciplinary measure. The school policy set out clearly that

> Permanent exclusion from school will only be invoked in an extreme or unresolvable situation, after every other possible expedient has been exhausted. The school will always seek to use the invaluable resources of the community through parental involvement, governor involvement and the support of community groups and associations to seek solutions to problems of student indiscipline.

However, the majority of the staff were still white and NAS/UWT, and exclusion was still central to their disciplinary approach. Particularly so, given the constant pro-exclusion declarations of their General Secretary, Nigel de Gruchy, and his opposition to the parental right to an exclusions appeal, which he described as hearings for 'irresponsible parents demanding the right to send their children to mainstream schools regardless of their offspring's behaviour.' He told BBC *Breakfast* in May 1998 that there were far too few 'disruptive' school students permanently excluded from school: another one hundred thousand should go, he exclaimed. Where they should go, he was less lucid about – the streets, the arcades, the McDonalds, the shopping centres like the new, huge and enticing Meadowhall in the graveyard of the Don Valley

174

steelworks? As long as they were out of the classroom and out of his members' hair, that was what mattered.

As a teacher, I could never support permanent exclusion: they very soon became dirty words for me and contrary to everything I believed in about school. I remember at Langdon Park the school had what it called a "sanctuary", an ex-caretaker's cottage next to the playground where, as an alternative to exclusion, seriously disruptive students would be sent for a few days and put under the supervision of a wonderfully and firmly warm local mother called Elsie, who knew many of the students and their families from the very streets where they lived. She had a transforming, calming, socialising and positive effect on them, and when they returned to classes they were frequently more reasonable and cooperative. And far from excluding difficult or absenting students, we would go out and find them in the different secret or not so secret places where they might go – adventure playgrounds, cafes, backstreet estate stairwells and lobbies.

And this wouldn't just be the teachers' task. I remember when a sometimes boisterous and provocative Jamaican boy called Stratford stopped coming to school. Some of his classmates were worried that he was getting into bad company, and one of them heard that he was spending his days at a sleazy billiard hall called Fat Cats along East India Dock Road, notorious as a hangout for petty criminals. So a group of my class and I turned up there one lunchtime. Although he seemed surprised and embarrassed yet also relieved, he came back to school with us, with all his classmates happy to see him again. After that, his attendence was good and he became one of the early birds, sitting with his mates in the classroom every morning, a good twenty minutes before the start of school. How could I forget all that?

At school, NAS/UWT members were not happy with the non-permanent exclusion policy. I was called to a CDT classroom where a teacher (who was a NAS/UWT member) and a student had become physical. According to the other students, the teacher had manhandled the fifteen-year-old Pakistani boy, who had pushed him away. The boy was actually a skilled amateur boxer who, if he had chosen to, could have done much more. I went quickly to the classroom and escorted the boy, who was quite restrained and affable, back to my office, where I phoned up his father. He agreed to come straight away to the school, to seek, without any belligerence, to resolve the problem with the teacher, who, on the advice of his local NAS/UWT district representative, declined to come. The father, meanwhile, was reasonable and helpful, and wanted to meet the teacher to calm the situation down and restore good relations. He waited patiently for the rest of the day, hoping for a meeting. But to no avail. The teacher would not talk to him, and NAS/UWT teachers within the school decided that they would not teach his son. The situation was eventually resolved, but for several days the boy worked quietly at a desk outside my room when he was due to be taught by a NAS/UWT teacher. I could, of course, have taken disciplinary action against these teachers for breach of contract, but I was a trade unionist myself and would not resort to such arbitrary action against fellow-trade unionists, even though I strongly opposed their action.

Meanwhile, as we pursued the non-permanent exclusion policy we had help and support from governors and local community organisations. I was not opposed to short-term temporary exclusion if something useful for the excluded student could emerge from it. One girl, for example, who was profoundly alienated from school life, was given a placement for a few days with an adult education initiative at the local African-Caribbean Enterprise Centre. She did well, was thought of positively there, and returned to the school a week later with much more constructive attitudes. A Somali boy who had been aggressive to his peers and rude to some colleagues was fostered for a week or so at the Somali Community Centre, where he listened to community elders and returned to the school with a new, more positive mindset. Governors were active in giving advice

176

and counselling to students who were approaching the brink of school life. What was becoming clear was that the community and its activists were the school's prime and most efficacious resource, which was a truth that the NAS/UWT members found difficult to accept. They believed that teachers and only teachers could organise and deliver discipline in the school, and that both community involvement and student self-organisation led to an overall situation where teachers were losing control. It was an authoritarian fear that without such absolute control, the school would descend into anarchy.

Around Sheffield the school was getting both a positive and negative reputation. The absence of permanent exclusions was praised within communities and among educational social workers, youth workers and educational psychologists. It had other more surprising supporters too. One morning I received an unsolicited phone call from an administrator in Attercliffe Police Station where a few weeks before I had been demonstrating alongside my students. Could the Chief Constable pay me a visit, she asked. Surprised, and wondering what I'd done now, I agreed, and the next morning the head of South Yorkshire Police walked into my office with polite and friendly greetings. I made him a coffee, and the conversation went something like this:

'So how can I help you?'
'I wanted to thank you.'
'Thank me? What for?'
'For your non-exclusion policy. You're making the lives of my officers a lot easier and less stressful.'
'What? How is that?'
'Instead of being on the streets or getting involved with crime or drugs, your students are in school where they should be.'
'Well, I agree with you there.'

I had heard much about about the South Yorkshire Police from the Miners' Strike and then Hillsborough, but this

177

Chief Constable, Richard Wells, who had been in office since 1990 was different to his predecessors. He had been openly critical of the way in which some police forces across Britain operated, within 'a culture of authoritarianism, defensiveness (and) excessive secrecy,' and was clearly trying to break away from that. He was also an opponent of school exclusion. He said that if we agreed, he could allot a community police officer to support the school's policy, and invited me to a meeting in a few days' time in Attercliffe Police Station to discuss the whole issue of school exclusion. The police colleague assigned with a brief to the school proved to have a very positive advisory influence. With the local drugs trade becoming more menacing, far from instilling fear and suspicion among students on the edge of school life, he spoke to them with empathy and insight, frequently persuading them from stepping over into criminal behaviour and preventing many personal tragedies. Ironically now, in 2020 as I write this account, many senior police officers are regularly giving television interviews about knife crime and arguing powerfully that school exclusion is one of the main reasons behind its growth across British inner cities. Wells' pioneering attitudes in the nineties have clearly taken root.

As Earl Marshal's reputation as a non-excluding school grew, ironically we began to attract parents across northeast Sheffield as a viable alternative to their excluded children being sent to exclusion centres or wandering the streets. We took in some of these, on the understanding with parents that they would take an active part in settling their children in school and would continue to be closely attached to their son's or daughter's progress. We also became much more vigilant about what was happening in the streets very close to the school. We had suspicions about particular houses in Owler Lane, just adjacent to the school grounds, where it seemed drugs were being distributed, and a local Yemeni cafe where it was thought dealers frequented and some of our truanting boys had been loitering. A Pakistani language teacher, Manzoor, who was a deeply committed Head of Year, interrupted them one morning and escorted them back to school, then returned to the cafe, spoke to the proprietor and a group of unemployed customers who had very little English. He offered to run a literacy class at the cafe and the owner and his regulars enthusiastically accepted. So he had turned a negative into an educational positive, and the run-down cafe became a surprising teaching venue with some unlikely students. For the community, the school began to be identified with such audacious initiatives.

Not the NAS/UWT though. In February 1995 one of their members had gone to the Sheffield *Star*. He was a supply teacher who had taught a few days at the school and had had some difficulties, claiming that he had found it necessary to lock himself in a room after being 'confronted by swearing pupils,' an incident he described as 'the worst experience' of his career. I had no reports of this and his claims were very short of detail. The *Star* had as its front-page headline next to my head and a photograph of the school, 'Teacher-bashing school probe.' The *Sheffield Telegraph* gave me the chance to reply three days later, and quoted me as saying: 'I feel very angry that our students, who are some of the finest I've ever come into contact with, have been caricatured in the press as if teachers have to lock themselves away from them.' With regard to difficult students, I added that 'we feel that by expelling them they will, without the constructive environment of the school, get into trouble with the drugs culture or with crime and become more of a worry within the community. Our approach is to keep them within school as much as we can and to work with them to change their behaviour. There are far too many students being excluded and wandering the streets.'

The 'teacher-bashing' article also exposed that David Blunkett MP, who had become Shadow Minister of Education, had sent a letter to the LEA 'expressing concern' about Earl Marshal, without sending a copy to me, as head-teacher of the school. This surprised me because I had

179

always supported Blunkett (he had been Council Leader when I was first appointed to Sheffield Education Department in 1984) and it was always considered good practice to send copies of letters of concern or complaint to the colleague who was the subject of criticism. Also, Blunkett was not the local MP for the Fir Vale district where Earl Marshal was sited. That was Richard Caborn, with whom I had a more positive relationship and had met him just a few months before when I accompanied a group of Earl Marshal students on a parliamentary visit to the House of Commons. Blunkett lived next door to a member of the Earl Marshal teaching staff who was particularly hostile to the non-exclusion policy so had received a negative perspective on the school and its policies. He was also intent on developing a strong relationship with the NAS/UWT, and had been warmly received by them at their last annual conference. So he became yet another powerful opponent, and one at the very heart of the system.

The Blunkett letter clearly caused some perturbation within the LEA and within the national media too. We were contacted by BBC's *Panorama,* who had decided they wanted to do a programme on the school, so topical and divisive had the issue of school exclusion become across Britain. They were determined to make the programme whether the school agreed or not and the hostile section of staff had been invited to appear. So we said we'd cooperate, although we were more than dubious about the programme-makers' motives. The interviewer was one Martin Bashir, who very soon was to make a worldwide name for himself as the interviewer of Princess Diana and who, in 2020 was investigated for using forged bank statements to persuade Diana to agree to the 1995 interview. In May 2021, ex-judge Lord Dyson's investigation into the Princess Diana *Panorama* programme, and Bashir's part in it, reported 'devious', 'dishonest' and 'deceitful' journalism. At the time I thought that Bashir, with his Pakistani roots, might have some empathy with the school's struggle against disproportionate black exclusions, but not a bit of it. He sat down in my office opposite Chairman of Governors Mike Atkins and myself, and although the camera seemed to be focusing on both of us, Mike was eliminated from the final cut. With no warning and without Mike or I having any opportunity to read its contents, Bashir produced a letter on camera from a group of teachers, in the main the familiar NAS/UWT members, complaining that they felt unsafe in the school and that the non-permanent exclusion policy was a dangerous development and a 'social experiment.' I said I knew nothing of this letter, hadn't read it and couldn't comment on it, and tried to justify the non-exclusion policy as best I could. But surprised and disturbed at the programme-makers' tactics, I don't think I was very convincing. I suppose I should have expected it.

The *Times Education Supplement* in its editorial of the 17 June 1994, entitled *Poor, black and ejected* in its characteristically patronising way, had found a novel comparison in describing me: 'Other headteachers regard Chris Searle, the Sheffield head who has vowed never to exclude a pupil, in much the same way as they would the Chinese surgeons who use acupuncture to anaesthetise patients undergoing open-heart surgery. They are perfectly prepared to believe it can work. But they would rather not risk it themselves.' The editorial continued: 'Searle's contention is that a 'climate of exclusions' has been created by the recession and the 1988 education reforms (the number of permanent exclusions leapt from 3000 in 1990-91 to 3822 in 1991-92, according to Department of Education figures). Children from home backgrounds and communities ravaged by unemployment and its attendant social ills are displaying aberrant behaviour just when schools are least capable of dealing with this additional problem. If a child misbehaves badly the temptation is to put *him* (boys are four times as likely to be excluded as girls), in the ejection seat and press the button.'

The imagery was crass and unhelpful, as the no-permanent exclusions policy of the school applied to all students, white and black, as did our welcoming approach to students excluded from other schools. As the school's NUT representative made clear in a letter to the Chief Education Officer:

> Before the present Head came to the school permanent exclusion was common as a way of dealing with children within the school and many staff expected this policy to be maintained. The new Head with the support of the governors proposed to explore other ways of resolving problems by broadening the school perspective to include as much community involvement as possible. This is a policy I support and regard as essential in an inner-city school catering for the educational and developmental needs of many different ethnic minority communities who now form the majority as well as the white working-class community that the school serves. Integral to this developmental strategy is the involvement of community groups who have been of effective support in devising solutions to problems.

As a Head of Year as well as an outstanding Science teacher; he was in a prime position to know well these problems and solutions, reminding the CEO of a number of key facts about the students in the year which he knew best. With regard to examination results he wrote: 'You will see a 100% plus improvement over the past year, pushing the school up five places in the league table.' He noted also that his year had the school's best attendance record for a decade, referring to Education Welfare Officer figures; an excellent exclusion rate from lessons record, and the additional point that: 'This year group also contained eleven students we accepted from other schools where they had been experiencing problems, all of whom achieved GCSE results, all of whom are now at college or on Youth Training schemes helping their year group reach the best 'staying on rate' we have ever achieved.' And he added as an afterword: 'As you see I prefer sustainable and checkable facts rather than hyperbole and innuendo. Are these not the primary indicators of the health of the school?'

As for the students, many of them gave me strong support the morning after the *Panorama* viewing. Almost all of them had watched it. None of the hostile colleagues had wanted to be openly identified, and the first shot of the programme showed their lower legs as they stepped out of a car. For many of the students, the day after was full of discussion of 'whose legs were they?' Or 'did you recognise the shoes?' Guesswork and sharp observation was all. Certainly it was a very strange and surreal day in the class-room.

Another consequence of the *Panorama* attack on inclusive education and our non-exclusion policy were the dozens of supportive letters and messages that I received from all over the country. From Sheffield they arrived from the Pakistani Muslim Centre, the Asian Welfare Centre, SADACCA, the Asian Youth Centre and the Rockingham Drugs Project which was tackling the serious drugs issue on the streets of Pitsmoor, all around the school. Other letters showed how much support there was all over Britain for our stand against exclusion. From Barnsley and Chesterfield to Ebbw Vale, Midlothian, County Durham, Bristol, Oldham and Stockport the solidarity poured in. Tim Brighouse, ex-Chief Education Officer of Birmingham, now Professor of Education at Keele University shared his support, as did the Bolton Institute, the Integration Alliance in South London and the Forum for Advancement of Education Therapy based in Ealing. There was even an apologetic letter from the BBC Current Affairs Department for excluding Chair of Governors Mike Atkins from the programme. Many nerves of indignation were touched, from the most surprising places.

As a result of the Blunkett letter and the local education authority's trepidation, in came OFSTED, preceded by LEA advisers, some of whom had been my ex-colleagues. One had a copy of the Blunkett letter which I had never seen. He showed it to me nervously, and although I was grateful to him for that, when I asked for a photocopy he declined, saying it would be more than his job was worth if it were discovered that he had shown it to me. Much more than a mere critique of the school's non-exclusion policies, it recommended my dismissal from the school. The Shadow

Minister was rehearsing his power, and also rehearsing his abuse of power. I understood now why he was so determined that the letter should not be made known to me and why my ex-colleague had been so fearful. And I also realised the extent of Blunkett's over-the-garden-fence knowledge of profoundly negative views of school life, for he had never visited the school.

As it turned out, the OFSTED inspectors were far more interested in curriculum issues provoked by the school than the workings of its non-exclusion policy. I had a particular argument with the History inspector who scornfully objected to the anti-imperialist posters framed and displayed in the school's resources area. They had photographs, prints and quotations about resistance to slavery, indentured labour and impoverished working conditions in the Caribbean, Africa and the Indian subcontinent during the centuries of British imperial rule. 'Wouldn't it be better to stress the peace and harmony in those eras,' he said. I asked him whether he had ever read Walter Rodney's books like *How Europe Underdeveloped Africa* or Richard Hart's *Slaves Who Abolished Slavery?* No, he didn't know of them, he admitted and hadn't heard of their authors. I wondered about his qualifications for the post, but I wasn't surprised.

In the event, we were put 'under special measures'. Of course, there was much to improve about the school and its examination results, and I was the first to admit it, but there was much to be proud of too. Then in the middle of all this, my Mancunian Deputy Headteacher colleague Eddie Coupe, suffered a heart attack and died. He was a popular and precious colleague who I had worked closely with for five years and the students took it very hard. We closed the school for his funeral and the Mother of God Catholic Church on Abbeydale Road was packed out by young Muslims many of whom had never been in a church before – there was hardly a practising Christian there, yet the church was full of love and respect for a teacher who had loved them all.

A group of senior Pakistani boys in smart suits, black ties and new shoes arrived at the Chesterfield cemetery for the burial in a shining, expensive-looking car. 'Where did you get it?' I asked, worried. 'We borrowed it Sir. We couldn't come to Mr Coupe's funeral without a car, could we? It wouldn't be reet. He would have expected it and we wanted to show respect.' I told them to take it back, quick, from wherever they had 'borrowed' it, or they'd be in serious bother. They said their fond farewells to Eddie and drove off regally back to Pitsmoor where they parked it back where they had found it. I don't think the real owner ever knew it had been taken. We never heard any more about it, anyway.

As the end of the Christmas term approached I told the Education Department that I had decided I was prepared to leave the school at the end of the Spring term, which would give the required three months notice. I thought that I had done what I could, that the school deserved new leadership and this would give the governors adequate time to find a successor. They agreed verbally, but I had little idea of what was transpiring in the rooms of the Leopold Street offices. On the day before the Christmas holidays began, I was summoned to the Department to meet the Chief Education Officer. On the way there I bought a *Star* at a Fir Vale newsagents to read on the bus. I read the morning headlines; I'd been sacked! The LEA had the grace to tell the press before they told me. At Leopold Street, where I had worked for six years, a retirement package was worked out between the Chief Education Officer and my NUT rep, and suddenly it was all over. I hardly knew the CEO. so I didn't have much to say to her. She thanked me, said goodbye and that was that. I was a gonner: excluded again!

I went home more than a little nonplussed. What the local education authority had done was unprecedented in Sheffield. They couldn't sack me directly because it was the task of the school governors who supported me, to make or end appointments. So in order to dismiss me the LEA had to remove the governors' delegated powers and take the powers themselves. So the governors had to be rendered powerless before the LEA could sack me. Which is what they did, rather than wait for Easter where all could be done respectfully and without rancour. Instead, the only black majority governing body ever in Sheffield, full of members with vital educational experience, community belongingness and administrative skills, was demeaned and dismissed. This was what made me so angry. I was a jobbing teacher, I knew I could find another job somewhere, as I always had. It didn't need to be a senior job, as long as it involved classroom teaching. But the governors worked out of love and service to school and their internationalist community; for no money and often with a lot of pain, heartache and frustration, and always with effort, honesty and committed integrity. And this is how those who controlled the schools in their city had treated them: as if they mattered for nothing.

The next morning I woke up at the usual time for school, to get there for a morning coffee and talk with the early birds at Shaheen's Café, when I realised that all that was over. As I sat with my breakfast, the telephone rang. 'Hello,' I said. The answer floored me: 'Hello Chris. This is Tony Benn, how can I help?' those last four words meant everything. I'd known Tony, who was MP for neighbouring Chesterfield, since 1989, when he wrote a very generous introduction to my memoir *Grenada Morning,* calling it 'a socialist classic.' He said had read about my dismissal this morning, and he wanted to lend his support. He suggested that he put an Early Day Motion in the Commons condemning my sacking and also embarrassing Blunkett. So he gathered together a cluster of the usual Labour left suspects to support the motion, which was eventually put to the House on 16 January:

Notices of Motions: 16th January 1996
CHRISTOPHER SEARLE
Mr Tony Benn
Mr Alan Simpson

Mr Jeremy Corbyn
Ms Diane Abbott
Alice Mahon
Mr Dennis Skinner
Mr Bernie Grant
Mr George Galloway
Mr Llew Smith
Mr John Austin Walker
Mr Brian Sedgemore
Mr Alan Meale
Mr Max Madden
Mr Peter Hain
Mr Robert N. Wareing
Mr Chris Mullin

That this House wishes to place on record its deep appreciation for the distinguished and committed life-long service
given by Christopher Searle to the cause of education, here
and world-wide; recognises his great contribution to
research into, and the practice of multi-cultural and anti-
racist teaching, creative writing and literacy, within a fully
comprehensive system of community education; notes his
many years of work in London, Grenada, Mozambique and
Sheffield during which he has inspired so many teachers
and students and demonstrated his capacity to win the
active and dedicated support of local people and the ethnic
communities, especially in deprived inner city areas;
greatly regrets the decision of the Sheffield Education
Committee to replace him as the Head Teacher of Earl
Marshal Comprehensive school against the opposition of a
majority of the governors of that school, and the decision,
by that authority, to strip those governors of their powers
so as to impose that decision; calls upon the Sheffield
Education Authority to restore to the governors of that
school their full powers to act; and expresses the hope that
Mr Searle's great talents and formidable abilities may be
fully used, in the future, for the benefit of education in
British society.

I had a strange few days, finding support in many unusual
contexts. When I went to buy a paper in WH Smith's in
town in Fargate, I found myself suddenly in the arms of a
Jamaican woman – I could tell from the accent, who hugged
me as she assured me of her support. I'd never met her

before. As I walked up my road, the 98 bus swept past, with a driver who would often take me to work early in the mornings shouting from his cab: 'It warn't reet duck, keep on fighting!' The *Star* reported that soon after the Christmas break a strike of a hundred students and a protest outside the school was called, with placards proclaiming 'Teachers helped to fail the school but the head got sacked' and 'Shame on the authorities.' In the *Yorkshire Post*, also on January 9th, I was quoted as saying: 'These are wonderful young people who are the hope of the world. They have a very strong sense of injustice. I can only thank them for their friendship and solidarity. However it is vital they return to the classroom and work towards achieving some marvellous exam results.'

As for the Governors, they put out a statement praising 'the confidence that has been built between the school and the Black Community,' criticising the 'Government's philosophy of judging schools through the distorting mirror of league tables rather than looking at the situation of the children as they come into the school and the progress that they make during their time at the school.' They went on to invoke the exclusion policy: 'The Authority is well aware of the school's policy on exclusion, and how the position was frequently undermined and challenged at every opportunity by a certain faction within the staff. At a time when there are nearly two hundred young people excluded from Sheffield schools, we could be forgiven for expecting acknowledgment and appreciation of our efforts to find a better way to respond to this challenging situation; and of the commitment demonstrated by Chris Searle in carrying out our policy whilst respecting the right of the teachers to challenge him. It is our contention that at times the actions of some of his colleagues was nothing short of sabotage. Again the Authority is aware of our concern at the way in which these were given credence by Senior Officers of the Education Department. At Earl Marshal we were beginning to re-establish a sense of regaining some accountability and the community itself establishing some control. The actions taken by the Authority at Earl Marshal ride rough shod over our efforts and leaves us feeling even more certain that the Authority's erstwhile commitment to Racial Equity and Social Justice was nothing more than a fashionable flirtation.'

The students were not silenced, and turned their attention to the crest of the three doves, for the local education authority, having displaced the governors and taken back total control of the school, appointed an acting head teacher from the ranks of the Advisory Service, where I had worked for six years. One of his prior acts was to discard the three doves from the school's emblem, and replace them with the former motif, the heraldic lions of the Duke of Norfolk. So the school reverted, in its symbolism, to its original aristocratic connections. A young Asian science teacher, together with a large group of senior students, led a protest about this, and letters of opposition were dispatched to the LEA, the press and using a stencil of the three doves and the book, the school walls around the entrance were painted with the ascending birds. The students campaigned for the reinstatement of the doves for the rest of the school year, and put forward a strongly-supported petition to the newly-appointed and predominantly white governors of the school, claiming that the doves represented:

All the communities of the school;
Equal opportunities for all races, colours, sexes, classes, abilities;
The power and strength of peace;
Learning;
That we, the pupils of Earl Marshal can fly high and achieve the best;
The Doves mean to many of us much more than the new crest.

And they appended a poem to the petition.

Learn to fly
Let your wings take you where you want to be.

Each and everyone has wings
It's just a matter of finding them
Let these doves fly as one.

The petition was rejected.

The Sheffield Black Community Forum, the unifying assembly of all of the city's black communities, organised a large public meeting in SADACCA to discuss the implications both of my removal and the withdrawal of delegation of Sheffield's only black majority school governing body. I was the main speaker. The meeting was packed out and full of angry and determined people. I talked about the profoundly institutionally racist way in which the LEA had removed the governors' delegation. It seemed to me then as it seems to me now, to be completely unconscionable, as if they were acting like the controllers of an apartheid state.

Meanwhile, my dear old friend Bill Moore had weighed in with his powerful intellect and historical truth. He was also an ex-teacher in wartime Nigeria and Sheffield and understood the crucial meaning of knowledge and internationalism. He devised a Sheffield-wide petition in my support and presented it to a Council Meeting with its large majority of Labour Councillors. It was a fine piece of writing, drawing comparison of Earl Marshal's internationalism with that of Sheffield's past history, from its campaigning against the slave trade to its support for the international Brigades in Spain and its twinning with Estelí in Nicaragua. He continued:

What Earl Marshal School has been doing is entirely in line with this great tradition. And the results show clearly in the books of children's writings: *Valley of Words, Lives of Love and Hope, School of the World* and *Heart of Sheffield.* If it's literacy you want, if it's articulateness you seek, especially from youngsters for many of whom English is a second language, you need go no further than these books.

Listen:
The school of the world is in the valley
The school of the world has different cultures

Its people have different languages
Its people have different life stories
The children all get along together in peace
The school of the world has children that come
From all different places in the world
The school of the world is a friendly school
The school of the world taught me everything I know
The school of the world taught me how to love others.

Amber

Again:

A teacher is not
Not an ordinary person
A teacher is one of the most important human beings on
earth
Important for me
Important for you
Important for everyone
The teacher is the base of everything
The teacher is the starter of everything.
The teacher is the only one who makes
doctors
    engineers
        mechanics
            lawyers
No matter what a student wants to be
No matter what his ambition is,
It can never become true without a teacher!
Teachers pass education to the student
You cannot become anything without a teacher,
That's why you should respect your teachers,
Because if you don't
Your ambition can never become true.
You should feel lucky that you have teachers,
Teachers who'll teach you
And make your ambition come true.
So without a teacher there's no life
For the teacher is like the sun,
And if there's no sun
There won't be any light –
And if there's no teacher
There won't be any education.
For teachers give you the light of education,

Teachers are a sea of education
And without them
You could imagine what your life could be like.

Nohman

What teacher would not be proud to receive such an unsolicited testimonial? These short samples tell it all, a school
embedded in the community, whose pupils are learning the
true way to a civilised life. We ask the Council to correct
the unhappy way Chris Searle was relieved of his post and
to give him the public commendation he has so richly
deserved.

Of course, they didn't. I went with Bill to the Council
meeting where the petition was up for discussion. There
was virtually no discussion: the Labour members were
whipped and all thirty-plus of them voted against the petition. There was not one single vote of support from them. I
came away downhearted, but wiser.

As I came home in the bus from that council meeting, my
mind was in turmoil, racked by self-doubt. How much had
I failed? Had I been too self-righteous and immodest about
my ideas and educational practice? I had been lucky. I'd
had a life exposed to all manner of experience and pedagogy
in many different contexts. I'd worked in the educational
cauldron of two revolutionary processes in Mozambique
and Grenada, and I learned so much from them. Most of my
colleagues had not had such vibrant learning experiences.
Some of them were locked in educational reticence and conservatism. Had I been too impatient, too self-assured –
even arrogant, in my ideas and practice?

That was twenty-five years ago and since then I have
often wondered why the Sheffield Labour Party seemed to
dislike me so much. When I arrived in the city in 1984 I was
a member of the Communist Party and although I was
appointed to a Labour education department, my long
experience in Liberation had showed me that progressive
spirits in both the Labour and Communist parties could
work together harmoniously and productively, with neither

rancour nor sectarianism. I also knew that the prime movers of my appointment were activists in Sheffield's black communities and without their pressure I would never have been appointed. But although I have always tried to find friendship with Labour people during all my thirty-six years in Sheffield, almost all my friends have been within the city's Black and refugee communities. In truth I have always felt closer to them than those in the Sheffield Labour establishment, always much more attuned to their life experiences and struggles. I don't know whether I was also suspected because I was a southerner and Londoner, but I have sometimes felt that. Yet I love Sheffield and its people and I have always found them warm and full of human feeling, whether I was in the classroom with their young people, playing cricket with them, sitting on buses with them, in hospitals with them or working close alongside them. Sheffielders have given me so much like Mike, Sue, Ahmed, Abdul and Bill, and Pedro – born in Valparaiso, Chile, imprisoned in Arica near the Peruvian frontier in the years after the 1973 fascist coup and finally released through constant pressure by Sheffield trade unionists. I never regret that I spent almost half my life here in a city that feels so different to London. When I go to London and then come back north again to Sheffield, I walk up the hill from the station, down through the Moor past the indoor market and the succession of low-budget and pound-saver shops, and then on to Sharrow and London Road, I can see and sense a poverty that is rarer in London: old and obese people staggering with plastic shopping bags of cheap food, or carefully and painfully with worn-out hips and knees climbing onto buses; young mothers with push-chairs searching for their fares and waiting with a stoical patience to find a bus that has a downstairs space for their prams; beggars and rough sleepers in the underpasses under St. Mary's Gate below; Chinese elders fending off the racist accusations and blame for coronavirus; elderly Pakistanis hobbling with sticks up the hill with the stands of Bramall Lane Football Ground forged in steel down the valley below them; the black and Asian youths stepping from the barber's shops with squarely-shaped hair; the cosmopolis of cafes and restaurants with the foods of the world; the understanding that in Sheffield neighbourhoods like this there is the statistical expectation that its residents will live a full decade less of life than those who live in the more leafy and affluent parts of the city.

It is a working class city with a wealthy outer ring and white suburban borders. It is England, still ravaged by class and extremes, where working people still love and struggle, and where I have been given so much.

As for the Earl Marshal young people, now suddenly my ex-students, I had this to say to the *Yorkshire Post* reporter, Chris Benfield, who came to interview me a month after my removal. On February 8th his article said about the sacking: 'It was certainly good for Labour's new image as the common-sense party. To the party's remaining idealists it was a shocking and cynical manoeuvre. But Searle says: 'I'll be back in some way. You cannot sacrifice ideas and a lot of people share mine. Schools have to be inclusive, not exclusive. The issues of inner-city education will never be resolved while we look on these remarkable and vibrant children as problems. Most know at least two cultures and languages well at twelve or thirteen. We must respect their intellectual power and their ambitions. They are much more world-aware than the ignorant people who talk about them and hand down insulting curriculum prescriptions.'

It's also what I think now, some quarter of a century later. The world will be theirs, and they will change it. But that is my long view of history talking, much inspired by my great drama hero, Bertolt Brecht, who told us in his play *The Caucasian Chalk Circle*, that I acted in nearly sixty years ago at school in Hornchurch, Essex that 'Long is not forever'. In Sheffield, the City Council, still Labour-led, got rid of me and its one school with a Black-majority governing body, got rid of Ahmed Gurnah and removed the Race Equality Unit and dispensed with the remarkable and

194

exemplary Mike Atkins. By the millennium they had wound up SUMES, even though seventy-five percent of its funding was coming from outside the City's coffers, directly from the Home Office – one hundred and sixty jobs. They even removed Sheffield's finest and fairest Chief Education Officer, Bill Walton, who had sanctioned and enabled the foundation and continuation of SUMES. Thus were the profoundly un-socialist policies of Sheffield City Council laid bare time after time, and such steps were but the harbingers of a new era of backwardness, decomprehensivisation, the withering away of the Local Education Authority itself and the rapid growth of academies, a form of educational privatisation first fostered by the Blairite Labour Party and local council compliance. It was for sure a long way from what I had found when I had arrived in Sheffield in 1984.

Shortly after the start of the new term, some of my closest colleagues at the school invited me back for a farewell assembly. There, in the Bill Owen Theatre, I thanked my old students for their friendship and loyalty, and a fourteen-year-old Yemeni student Yahya, read his poem which had been published in *Heart of Sheffield*. He had given it a simple title; *Unity* he called it.

It means people are together
But where is unity?
When I watch the TV
When I listen to the radio
I hear about drugs.
When I go to school
I hear somebody fighting somebody.
No! No! No!
This is not unity.
It's not about fighting
Or being the strongest in the school.
No! No! No!
Its about being clever with your brains
Not with your muscles.
You and me and she and we,
We're not enemies!
We can stop the fighting,
Stop the bullies with our brains!

195

We have brains, we can stop them,
I can, you can, we can
With our brains!

Yahya's words and message resonated with all of us, and he followed his poem by one in Arabic from one of my dearest poets whose poetry we had studied in English translation in our classes, the Palestinian laureate Mahmoud Darwish. I couldn't understand the words but one of my Arabic-speaking colleagues whispered in my ear

Pupils vent their anger at the loss of their popular headmaster Chris Searle

Pupils boycott classes

PUPILS boycotted classes to protest against the sacking of Earl Marshal School headteacher Chris Searle.

Protesters claimed 100 pupils joined in the protest after claiming they were misled about the decision to axe Mr Searle.

Protest leader and pupil Yousaf Mohammed, aged 16, said pupils were told Mr Searle left of his own free will.

"The teachers lied to us and we only found out the truth through The Star. We at least want him to be allowed to come back and say goodbye because he was a popular teacher.

"We think he's been badly treated and carried the can for the school being classed a failure." The pupils carried placards saying: "Teachers helped to fail the school but the head got sacked" and "Shame on the authorities."

BY ROB HOLLINGWORTH

Yousaf added the protest could continue throughout the week unless an explanation was given.

Acting head Roy Spooner was unavailable

Yousaf Mohammed

for comment yesterday, but has admitted the school is now on its last chance after being dubbed a failure last summer by inspectors.

Mr Spooner added: "The education department wouldn't have taken the action it did if that wasn't the reality of the situation."

Governors at the school demanded an explanation of why they had key powers removed. They are also demanding to be fully involved in the selection of a new head.

A majority of governors are threatening to resign if their demands are not met and claim the community will lose faith in the school if that happens.

Sheffield *Star*: 9 January, 1996

Pupils quit lessons in support of sacked head

Jillian Ward

PUPILS from a school at the centre of a race-row walked out of lessons yesterday in protest at the sacking of its headteacher.

About 70 children from Earl Marshal secondary school in Sheffield staged a demonstration outside the gates, distributing leaflets which accused staff of betraying former head Chris Searle.

Tensions at the school, which has been the subject of two highly critical official reports, are already running high after a statement made last week by seven black governors branding Sheffield Council racist.

They are furious at the decision taken last month by education officials to remove Mr Searle and strip the governing body of key powers without any consultation.

Earl Marshal is the only school in Sheffield which has a majority of black members on the governing body.

Youngsters at yesterday's demonstration called for the return of Mr Searle, who was already due to take early retirement from the school in April.

He has already supported the black governors and accused Sheffield Council of racist behaviour.

Last week black governors accused some of the teaching staff at Earl Marshal of deliberately "sabotaging" some of Mr Searle's management policies, especially his decision not to exclude disruptive or violent pupils.

An education department official said: "Everyone at the school is trying to work very hard to overcome any problems we have had.

"The acting head teacher and senior staff hope to meet with some of the youngsters today to discuss the situation."

Sheffield Education Authority said Mr Searle had been invited to return to the school to say an official goodbye to staff and pupils. He was sacked on the final day of the winter term.

Yesterday Mr Searle said he was touched by the show of feeling for his departure by pupils, but urged them to return to lessons today.

"These are wonderful young people who are the hope of the world.

"They have a very strong sense of injustice. I can only thank them for their friendship and solidarity.

"However, it is vital they return to the classroom and work towards achieving some marvellous exam results.

"I should like to go back to the school and say goodbye to them myself, sometime in the near future."

Earl Marshal yesterday remained open for the majority of the 530 pupils and lessons are expected to continue as normal today.

Yorkshire Post: 9 January, 1996

Where should the birds fly
After the last sky?

Shafina, a vivacious Pakistani girl who was constantly in trouble and a very frequent visitor to my office, suddenly stood before me with a large bouquet. I'd never been given flowers before and felt deeply moved. I left the school for the last time and walked down to Fir Vale, catching the bus back to the city centre, walked up Fargate almost in a trance, covered by the scent of roses, and transported by marvellously vibrant young people, most of whom after years of closeness, I would never see again.

Chapter 7
Pitsmoor to Tyendinaga

I don't think I could have found a place more different to Pitsmoor and Fir Vale than Cambridge, where I found my next post. I was invited to work for the university's Institute of Education as a Research Fellow, investigating alternatives to school exclusion. It was a temporary post, with promises of it eventually becoming permanent, but somehow it wasn't for me, I couldn't really identify with the university's elitist ambiance and I have never really seen myself as an academic. I needed to teach. Even at Earl Marshal I had kept a strong classroom teaching commitment and described myself to OFSTED (much to their chagrin) as 'fundamentally a teacher with extra responsibilities, not a manager,' which had been another cross against me. So when a post was advertised at Goldsmiths' College in a deeply working-class neighbourhood of South London, as a teacher educator in charge of the teaching of English, I successfully applied for it. It had been Professor James Britton, a Professor of Education at Goldsmiths' who had written back so positively and warmly when we had published *Stepney Words* in 1971 and sent him a copy, and had invited me to have coffee and a discussion about children's poetry with him in his office on Lewisham Way. So I saw that as a happy omen when I applied, and soon after the new Professor of Education became Clyde Chitty, a champion of comprehensive schools and ex-colleague of the foremost socialist education scholar and writer, Brian Simon. So just a few months after being bundled out of Earl Marshal so ruthlessly, I felt like a lucky man. I became a weekly commuter, returning to Sheffield every weekend.

I had some lively, humorous and committed student teachers too, and it took me back to the teacher training I did in Grenada. But now there were no Caribbean villages and schools with breadfruit and mango trees in their yards. The students had placements in large South London comprehensives like Crown Woods, Plumstead Manor, Deptford Green and Abbey Wood, and it wasn't an easy apprenticeship for them, as I found as I did my rounds of classroom visits. Some of these schools were huge, nothing like the relatively small 600-pupil roll of Earl Marshal, and it was easy for young or inexperienced teachers to feel lost and alienated. Which was certainly not how I felt on my teaching visits to the wonderful Gayhurst Primary School next to London Fields in Hackney, where I worked on my finale of Young World Books, helping to produce a beautifully vibrant anthology with its ten and eleven year-old pupils: *Hackney: The Borough of Life*. This was east London and its children a decade and a half after I had last taught here. There were new communities – Bosnians, Albanians, Congolese, Brazilians, an Earl Marshal of children, and also a warmth full of social love and unity. As one of the school's young poets put it in a praise song to her school:

Gayhurst School is cool
All the children of the world are welcome
Yellow skirted daffodils in London Fields

As the book was launched with the whole school present, Michael Rosen read some poems, Jeremy Corbyn as Chair of Liberation was a surprise guest and a boy called Lazar Zindovic read his poem called *Hackney* with tremendous spirit and gusto:

The borough of life
Where people laugh,
Where people party,
Where people play,
Where people drink.

The borough of comedy;
We've got the Empire and the Ocean,
We've got jokes in the playground,
We've got drunk men in the streets.

The borough of people
Where everyone's happy,
Where everyone's friendly,
Where everyone's generous,
Where everyone's funky.

The borough of culture; we are black,
We are white
We are mixed,
We are a community.

The borough of the world;
We are from Yugoslavia,
We are from Nigeria
We are from Jamaica,
We are from Turkey,
We are from all over the world.

The borough of the parks;
We've got London Fields,
We've got Hackney Downs,
We've got Clissold Park,
We've got Victoria Park.

The borough of the streets;
Where people can't play,
Where children can't hang around,
We children can't go anywhere by ourselves.

The borough of my dreams;
Clean streets,
No racism,
No drugs
I WANT ALL OF US TO BE A COMMUNITY

It could have been Pitsmoor that he was writing about, for the images were the same and the problems as a mirror to the streets around Earl Marshal, more than two hundred miles away in another great city. And the hopes and dreams of the children were similar too, but with a different London argot. The universe of children's poetry was everywhere.

I worked and wrote hard during my Goldsmiths' years. I produced four books. One was *None but Our Words*, a study of what I called *Critical Literacy in Classroom and Community* from *Stepney Words to Earl Marshal*. That school was my main focus in *Living Community, Living School*, and I wrote about both physical exclusion from school and curriculum exclusion in *An Exclusive Education: Race, Class and Exclusion in British Schools*. I was thrilled when my education hero, Brian Simon, wrote a back cover statement calling it 'A well-documented, challenging and striking read, and his critique of the National Curriculum is substantial and first class.' I also wrote my only book on cricket, *Pitch of Life* with an introduction by the brilliant American cricketing sage, Mike Marqusee, and many articles on jazz for the *Morning Star*, for which I became jazz correspondent, as well as weekly book review articles for the paper under the pseudonym of *The Bookie*. I also organised, in conjunction with Lewisham Teachers Association of the NUT. a tribute conference to Blair, twenty years after his murder. Speakers included the poet Benjamin Zephaniah, Colin Prescod from the Institute of Race Relations and speakers from the campaigns around the racist murders of Stephen Lawrence and Ricky Reel. A young Lewisham teacher, Alison Moore who had been attacked by racists in a local South London street, gave a particularly moving talk, and Caroline and Tony Benn were there to wind up the proceedings. We called the day *Blair Peach Lives!* – as he still does for all of us.

The Art Education Lecturer, Paul Dash, became a special friend. Born in Barbados in 1946, he migrated to Oxford to be with his family in 1957. Not to the 'City of Spires', but to the working class neighbourhood of Cowley, where his father worked in the Morris motor factory.

Paul found himself in a no-hopers secondary modern school, subject to the English educational racism at its worst. In defiance of the racist culture pitted against him, he achieved an inspiring life in teaching and teacher education, as well as becoming a pioneering figure in the Caribbean Artists Movement, with his paintings eventually exhibited in the Royal Academy and the Tate. He contributed a powerful cover drawing for my book on exclusions, *An Exclusive Education*, and I wrote an introduction to his compelling autobiography, *Foreday Morning*.

An Exclusive Education

Race, class and exclusion in British schools

Chris Searle

By 1999 I had become active within the anti-racist cricket movement Hit Racism for Six, a conception of Mike Marqusee, author of the brilliant analysis of the English cricket scene, *Anyone but England*. I contributed two articles to the first issue of their campaigning journal. Yet suddenly, I found myself deeply involved in a grotesque racist incident in football in June 2000 involving a group of Leeds United players who chased a young Pakistani from Rotherham, Sarfraz Najeib, through Leeds city centre, attacked and severely injured him, still kicking him as he lay on the street with a broken leg, broken nose and a serious bite on his cheek; injuries all inflicted by the footballers. Sarfraz' father owned a takeaway in Sheffield, and when a campaign was launched in support of his son, his car's tyres were slashed, he was racially abused and threatened at his workplaces and became the target of a series of racist incidents. When the case came to court, several Leeds players were arraigned, including prominent first team players Lee Bowyer and Jonathan Woodgate. Another player, Paul Clifford, was sentenced to six years for inflicting the bite, while Woodgate and Bowyer got off lightly, Woodgate receiving 100 hours community service and Bowyer was acquitted, although the judge described his testimony as 'littered with lies.' Bowyer had previously been involved directly in violent racism. In September 1996, three months after he joined Leeds United, the *Daily*

Mail had reported that he, together with others had been involved in an attack on Asian staff at a McDonald's on the Isle of Dogs, East London, when a Bangladeshi worker, Shamsul Ali, was on the receiving end of a violent rant by Bowyer, who threw the cheeseburger Shamsul had served him to the ground, exclaiming that he wouldn't eat anything served to him by a 'fucking Paki,' hurling chairs and causing an affray for which he had been fined £4,500 – half a week's wages for him.

Bowyer's racism was part and parcel of the football club's culture. Bowyer had been awarded 'Player of the Year' status and the club's chairman, Peter Ridsdale sanctioned £2m legal fees and chauffeur-driven rides to court for the player-defendants during the Safraz Najeib hearings. In May 2002 at the club's award ceremony, the so called 'comedian,' Stan Boardman, was the guest entertainer. On the front pages of the *Daily Mirror* of May 2, 2002, beside the headline 'Leeds Race Outrage,' the paper reported that Boardman cracked jokes about 'murdering an Indian' and when an Asian supporter Steven Thomas called him a 'disgrace,' his riposte was: 'Fucking hell, I'm being heckled by Pakis now!'

I had been invited as a speaker to the *Football, Citizenship and Anti-racism* conference in May 2002 at Old Trafford, the stadium home of Manchester United Football Club, organised by Let's Kick Racism Out of Football. The conference's brochure cover displayed an inspiring colour photograph of the great Brazilian striker, Pele and the 1966 World Cup winning England captain Bobby Moore – against whom I had played cricket as an Essex school boy – embracing and exchanging shirts after the 1970 Mexico World Cup match at Guadalajara. In my speech I concentrated on the racist culture at Leeds United, a team I had once supported during my three university years in the city during the mid-sixties. This created both much support, and indignant denials by Leeds United, and resulted in me being invited to the club's stadium at Elland Road, Leeds, to discuss what I had said, and to seek to convince me how

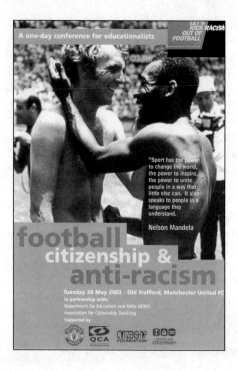

A one-day conference for educationalists

LET'S KICK RACISM OUT OF FOOTBALL

"Sport has the power to change the world, the power to inspire, the power to unite people in a way that little else can. It also speaks to people in a language they understand.

Nelson Mandela

football citizenship & anti-racism

Tuesday 28 May 2002 - Old Trafford, Manchester United FC
In partnership with:
Department for Education and Skills (DfES)
Association for Citizenship Teaching
Supported by:
QCA
CITIZENSHIP FOUNDATION
INSTITUTE FOR CITIZENSHIP

wrong I was. I was neither convinced nor impressed by their testimony or the way they avoided any self-criticism for their players' behaviour and racist violence against Sarfraz. As I left, I remember thinking: 'This is not going to change without mass organisation by players and supporters, and a complete change in the clubs' modes of ownership and management.' And I reflected too that all this racism had taken place in cities where I had lived, studied and worked – Leeds, East London, Sheffield, and how it was not simply a local outbreak, but a national disgrace with footballers like Bowyer and Woodgate with their noxious racist actions behind them, becoming managers of leading Championship clubs, Charlton Athletic and Middlesbrough respectively, while talented prospective Black managers, ignored, unappointed and repudiated, are still such a football rarity.

I was back playing cricket again, this time for my old Sheffield club, at their park ground, Millhouses, now opening the batting and an occasional seam bowler, and never far from my usual place in the field, scouring the Third Man boundary. We played competitive and needle matches against local works teams like EMGAS, in their tiny, crater-like ground, Sheffield Co-op or Sheffield Transport, and it was always heartening to know and feel that cricket in South Yorkshire was much more a working class sport than I had known in the Essex suburbs. One of the season's keenest matches was against Sheffield Caribbean at their Ecclesfield ground, their team full of West Indian talent still inspired by an epoch when their national team was mastering the cricket world, with quick bowlers like Andy Roberts, Malcolm Marshall, Joel Garner and Michael Holding, and the astonishing batting prowess of Viv Richards, Gordon Greenidge, Clive Lloyd and Desmond Haynes.

Then there was also the joy of playing in the North Derbyshire League in some idyllic Peak District grounds like the sloping turf of Hathersage, two valley grounds with the River Derwent flowing past its boundaries, as at Grindleford and Baslow looking up to Chatsworth House. Or the tiniest of grounds like Calver, about twice the size of a tennis court where almost every forceful air-shot meant a six, yet where pitches were loved and cared for with reverence and pride, making me feel as if I was enjoying a slice of heaven every summer Saturday afternoon. As the years went by our team began to consist of a combination of fathers and teenage sons, often with four or five pairs playing together. As our boy Daniel developed into the League's quickest opening bowler, I could only watch in wonder and pride from Third Man as his lightning bowling broke opposing batsmen's stumps and found flying edges grasped and hung onto by the slips.

I worked at Goldsmiths' for five years, but I never left Sheffield. Our children were still at school there so rather than move, I commuted, returning for weekends to Sheffield. It wasn't a situation I liked, so when Abdul Shaif, ex-Earl Marshal governor and Chair of the Yemeni Community Association asked me to come and work for them as a teacher at their Centre in Attercliffe, it was a tempting offer not to be refused, particularly as Adult Education was a new venture for me and I was working for and with a Sheffield community which I knew, admired and loved.

It was a multifarious job, and every part of it I enjoyed. I taught English as a second language to newly-arrived Yemenis, Iraqis, Iranians, Syrians and Afghans, where I also learned much about their lives and nations. I supported and advised young Yemenis in their efforts to establish a viable youth association, and I taught English to one of the most remarkable classes I have ever taught. They had an average age of 76 and were all retired steelworkers who had arrived as part of the first wave of Yemeni migrants in the Fifties and Sixties, and had, to a man, been plunged straight into the heat and jeopardy of the Don Valley's great steelworks.

In the large attic room of the terraced house in Burngreave Road, Pitsmoor, originally bought collectively by the first generation of Yemeni steelworkers as their first community centre, a basic classroom was constructed. Up the steep stairs, helped by their sticks and their hearing aids in the ears, twenty-two old men, some well into their eighties, would climb and stagger, laughing, puffing and spluttering. This was my class of keen and often boisterous, veteran ex-steelworkers determined, and for many it was the first opportunity in their life, to at last learn English, in a formal sense. I loved this class – always good humoured, brotherly and habitually punctual – they were used to losing a full fifteen minutes pay if they were a few seconds late for their steelworks shifts. They began steelmaking lives in the Fifties and Sixties as unskilled foundry workers –'slingers' they were called, doing the dirtiest and most dangerous of jobs in the foundries, often for 65-75 hours a

207

Veterans still a class act

Sheffield *Star*: 8 April, 2004

Late learner: One of the elderly students in the English class

Class mates: Teacher Chris Searle with some of his students, from left, Muthana Asad, Awadh Gobran, Ali Naher, Obadi Saleh, Saleh Muthana and Mohammed Ali

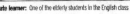

Picture: Andrew Partridge

Ex-steelmen in their 80s grabbing the chance to learn

By Lucy Ashton

FORMER steelworkers from Sheffield's Yemeni community are to appear on national radio talking about their jobs and lives.

The men are all now aged in their 70s and 80s but still attend daily classes at Sheffield Yemeni Community Association to improve their English.

They will feature on a Radio 4 programme called Born in Yemen, Forged in Sheffield which will be broadcast on Monday April 19 at 11.30am. The programme is part of a series of documentaries by Alan Dein about aspects of British life.

Chris Searle, an English teacher at the Community Association, said it was remarkable that the men were still learning as pensioners.

He said: "They are all ex-steelworkers from the Yemeni community and still come to school every day.

"They are trying to develop their English because they were never given classes when they arrived and have never been taught formal English.

"We have 20 regular class members and some are in their 80s. This is the first organised teaching they have ever had and it's quite unique."

The men came to Sheffield in the 1950s to find work.

Chris added: "They had a remarkable journey. They came from Yemen and didn't speak any English but went straight into heavy industry in Sheffield.

"They became very much a forgotten community because they sent most of their money home to look after their family.

"They lived in terraced housing and didn't spend much on themselves. Even at this age though they are still willing to learn."

week to earn money to send as remittances back to their families in Yemen. They lived in unheated terrace houses, eating tuna and rice and meeting socially in Arab cafes in Attercliffe and Burngreave, with regular worship in local mosques. In the final decades of Sheffield's steel industry, they were invaluable assets to its survival.

Our classes became community epics of storytelling. They loved their stories of farmwork childhoods in Yemen, of the voyage from Aden or Djibouti to Italy, then the overland passage to Dover, of their arrival and first months in Sheffield. We developed a 'pedagogy of story' together. I would read out, correct and type up their narratives which would lead to another and another, so that we studied and learned in a forest of stories. And we would sing. I would teach them songs and sometimes change the words to give them more meaning. They loved *When You're Smiling*, which I used to teach the present continuous or the beloved *We'll Meet Again* as an example of the future tense. We would sing *The White Cliffs of Dover* which they remembered well as the first view of England that they had seen when they first arrived. The words had a powerful effect too:

> There'll be love and laughter
> And peace ever after,
> Tomorrow, when the world is free!

We learned *Maybe it's Because I'm a Londoner* but changed the last word to 'Sheffielder' because they loved the city so much, and to Woody Guthrie's *This Land is Your Land* we gave a new chorus:

> This land is your land
> This land is my land
> From the streets of London
> To the hills of Sheffield,
> From Attercliffe Common
> To the River Don's water,
> This land was made for you and me.

We had minibus trips out too. I remember we went to Whitby for the day, singing as we travelled, eating fish and chips on the quay and as the Yemeni veterans reached the end of the long stone jetty, they decided to face Mecca, fall on their knees and pray; a dozen or so old men in sandals and with sticks, much to the bemusement of passers-by and tourists.

The brilliant BBC radio documentary-maker Alan Dein, made a programme about them. He quoted Menasser who told him that when he arrived in Sheffield fifty years before both his managers and the Job Centre gave him no help with English: 'I was told I'm here to work, not learn. 'Don't worry about school,' they said, 'just work!' And Obadi, 81 years old told *The Guardian,* who wrote a feature on the class: 'We want to know everything! When I see my doctor, when I sign my insurance, I want to know how to speak. When I was in the factory, I go from house to work, from work to house, and there is no time to learn. Because of coming here, because of our teacher Chris, sometimes life is easier.' But it took some time getting used to their unique way of speaking English. They spoke with great volume – their loud words were to make sure they could be heard in the huge noise and hammers of the foundries and rolling mills. Many of them were all but deaf, and the Yemeni Community Association had organised a successful campaign against the steel companies to get them compensation. And secondly, as I told *The Guardian*: 'They use the imperative mood all the time, and that's because they were used to having orders loudly barked out to them all the time. I had to get used to that – it's startling, because they talk in commands!' and yet they were among the kindest and gentlest students I had ever taught: 'They're an example to anyone who wants to learn. That a group of twenty men with an average age of 76 can study and improve their English, and do so with such keenness and good humour, is an example to all students in this country. In that sense, they make a nonsense of old age, because their spirit is full of youth and fire.'

The pedagogy of story worked with a true dynamic. Story begat story. Here was Omairat:

There were no English classes for us, we had to learn our new words from the gaffers in the foundries and rolling mills and try to understand what they shouted at us.

And it was very dangerous work too. We couldn't read any of the safety notices or warnings they had in the steelworks when we first came. There were some bad accidents because we couldn't read the instructions. It wouldn't be allowed now.

I remember in the rolling mill when a rod of steel went through a Yemeni's leg because he didn't know what to do. They took him to hospital and they cut off his leg. He didn't work again in any steelworks.

These classes we have now, even though we're retired and old, are the first we've ever had, and they're organised by our own community. The State gave us nothing, even though some of us have been in Sheffield and paid our taxes and rates for fifty years.

And once they started, the stories of their journeys were unstoppable. Here was Nasser:

When I came to England in 1956 I travelled on an Italian ship. We couldn't understand the menu in the ship's restaurant and we didn't want to eat any pork, so to make sure, all we ate were eggs. Every day, only eggs! Eggs for breakfast, eggs for lunch, eggs for dinner, eggs for supper too! Only eggs, eggs, eggs, all the way to Genoa. How I wished for a good lamb dinner, like I used to have in my home village!

And Saleh responded:

When I arrived Sheffield station from London after I left the ship at Tilbury, I didn't know anyone and I didn't know where to go.

A taxi driver said, 'Try Attercliffe. I think there are some Arabs there,' but I didn't understand him. He took me to Attercliffe then to Darnall. He started to knock on the doors of the houses along one street to see if the people who lived there would rent me a room.

On the eleventh house where he knocked a lady called Doreen opened the door. 'He can stay with me, he's welcome,' I found out later she said. So I moved into that house.

It was near the Brown Bailey steelworks. So later that first night I went there to ask for a job. And I got a job there in the middle of the night! When I came back to Doreen's house she was angry and worried because I didn't tell her where I went. She even slapped me because she was so upset and cared for me.

'Where did you go all night?' she shouted. 'I found a job!' I shouted back happily in Arabic. I stayed for six months with Doreen; she always looked after me and even took care of my wages for me. She was a very honest woman.

They talked and wrote about coming to England during the mid-fifties, the era of anti-Arab racism around the British invasion of Suez and they also told of the racism of early foundry days:

Every day when we arrived and clocked in, one of the white steelworkers said to my friend from my village, 'Hello, black bastard!' He said this out loud every day for the first week. We asked him to stop, but he carried on saying it every morning, 'Hello, black bastard.'

So my friend and I went to the gaffer to complain about this daily insult. He said, 'Well that's what you are, a black bastard. It's true, isn't it?' And he did nothing to stop it.

So my friend gave the worker a warning himself in the little English he had. 'I'll give you a week to stop. If you carry on with this insult week after week, then I will have to take action.' But every day he started with the same words. He did not stop.

So after a week my friend was true to his word. He brought in a knife and cut the man who called him 'black bastard.' And he never called him that again.

The racism story created a flurry of narrative rejoinders, including this one, which provoked a storm of laughter across the attic room:

I worked with my cousin and two other Yemenis as crane drivers. I worked on a twelve hour shift from six o'clock in the morning to six o'clock in the evening, and I had to take a pot in the crane to piss into, because we were up there so long. I used to throw the piss out of the crane down over the workers who didn't like us Arabs. We were high up above the factory floor, and there was a lot of smoke and it was very hot up there.

This story spurred a story with a contrary theme:

There were a lot of us Yemenis working there, and we were friendly with the English steelworkers. We all talked, laughed and joked together. Then we went on strike together for better pay. The managers at first refused to recognise our union, and one manager thought maybe he could get at us Yemenis, and he came to my house when I was on strike to try to persuade me to come back to work. But we stayed out for another two weeks, and they raised our pay, and only then we came back.

And then more stories with the union as protagonist:

When I arrived in 1956, I found that in our factory the union wasn't very strong and the gaffers did almost what they wanted with us. They told us we had to work on many jobs, one after the other, not just on one. When we finished work on one machine, they said we must move on, straight away, to another job. They got a lot of work out of us all right, for the same low pay. If we refused to move on to the next job, they threatened to send us home or to sack us.

Sometimes they made us work for sixteen hours at one time until we were nearly too tired to stand up. Then we had to go home to cook and sleep and then come back again for another double shift.

It was very hard work, and so hot too all the time. Hotter even than Aden! But after a time the union stopped all this pressure and it became better for us.

One after another, almost ceaselessly the stories came during those marvellous Pitsmoor mornings. I'd never been so happy in a classroom, and reading back over some of the press cuttings on the time, I came upon this extract from the *Sheffield Telegraph*, when I was telling their journalist about one of the memorable moments:

I said recently: 'Today we're going to learn about adjectives,' Chris remembers. 'And one of them said, 'Oh that's

213

where I used to work.' I had to think for a moment. 'No, not Attercliffe, Ali! Adjectives!'

They used to bring me rice, mutton, sticks of rhubarb. They're almost all gone now: Yemenis all, Sheffielders all! But the brave stories of their migration are to be found, with all their humanity and humour, in my son Kevin's book *From Farms to Foundries: An Arab Community in Industrial Britain* (Peter Lang Publishers).

In 2004 I was invited to become a Visiting Professor at the University of York in Toronto, at Atkinson College which specialised in courses for mature students who were returning to education often after years of work in offices, shops, fast-food places, warehouses and call centres, postal vans and nurseries. I spent a wonderful first year there, so much so that they invited me back for another. My courses concentrated on childhood and education, with *The School and Fiction* featuring extracts from some of the great novels and short stories about different modes of schooling from *Tom Brown's Schooldays* and Joyce's *Portrait of the Artist* to James Matthews' South African story *The Park*, Ghassan Kanafani's Palestinian story *The Slope*, David Mulwa's Kenyan novel *Master and Servant*, R.K. Narayan's Indian pre-independence novel, *Swami and Friends* and Merle Hodge's novel of a girl in Trinidad, *Crick Crack Monkey*. Pepetela's *Ngunga's Adventures* was in there too with Austin Clarke's Barbadian memoir *Growing Up Stupid Under The Union Jack* and Billy Colvill's play of the 1911 school strikes in East London, *Fall in and Follow Me*, with South Yorkshireman Barry Hines' *A Kestrel for a Knave* and *The Diary of Anne Frank* with Vargas Llosa's Peruvian tale of officer cadets, *The Leaders*. Rita Joe's Native Canadian poetry was studied too with that of the Palestinian Mahmoud Darwish and Mildred D. Taylor's novel of a Mississippi childhood, *Roll of Thunder, Hear My Cry* with Joan Riley's tale of a Jamaican girl in a London school, *The Unbelonging* and Ha Jin's Chinese story, *In the Kindergarten*. One of the assignments was for the students to write a creative or autobiographical piece about their own schooling. So the stories of childhood in Korea, India, Romania, St. Lucia, China, Sri Lanka, Pakistan, Italy and many other countries of origin in this most diverse and internationalist city came together in two anthologies published by the university. The first was *Cosmopolis, Toronto*, the second concentrated on the life stories and extraordinary journeys of the students' parents and grandparents. I called it *Toronto Generations* and it was akin to the structure of the anthology of *Lives of Love and Hope*, for these were men and women from everywhere. From Alexandria, Dar-es-Salaam, Asyaboon in Eastern Iran, Lebanon, Arima in Trinidad, China, Guyana, Sicily, Ho Chi Minh City. They told stories of a Ukrainian woman destined for domestic drudgery fleeing from life in Saskatchewan; a Jewish Canadian soldier from Toronto among the first Allied troops to arrive in and liberate Belsen in 1945; a Greek grandmother remembering a childhood confrontation with a Nazi soldier in her birth village; an illiterate Ghanaian grandmother teaching her granddaughter to count using stitching on her Kente cloth; a Caribbean granddaughter remembering her grandmother who mothered her in the small village of South Hill, Anguilla. As the students wrote these life stories, many of them in their thirties and forties – one was in her sixties, the signal truth of educational late development became clearer and clearer to me. I always knew it as I was a product of it myself. Life itself was education, was learning. These students were studying for a first degree at a time in their lives when school was a distant memory in many faraway places and they were emulating in study the long-time achievements of their parents' and grandparents' lives, as the foundation of new insight and learning in another country, a great new city, which would be the fresh landscape of their lives. This was my second sojourn in Canada. In 1966 I had learned a lot: now in 2005–07 I knew I was learning even more and it was my students who were my teachers.

215

I hadn't been in Toronto since 1967. I had arrived in its neighbouring city, Hamilton, as a landed immigrant and an M.A. student and spent a lot of time in Toronto. Then, it seemed like a much whiter city. There were many families from Italy, Greece and many European nations, but four decades on it had changed enormously and become one of the great internationalist cities of the world. It was as if everyone from everywhere was there and the students of York University manifested that truth with a pride and passion.

One of my closest colleagues became Bonita Lawrence, a Professor of Indigenous Studies and of native Canadian, Mi'kmaq heritage. We had much in common as she had lived in East London in the 1970s when I was teaching there. We didn't know each other then, yet it somehow seemed that we did as we recalled people and places in Mile End, Limehouse and Stepney that we both knew in different yet related ways. When the university year ended, she helped me organise a period of voluntary teaching at the Mohawk reservation school in Tyendinaga, Eastern Ontario, a very different setting to York University. I said I'd teach the elementary school-aged children there some creative writing, and the school's teachers said they'd be happy to have me.

Ever since I began to teach creative writing in my classrooms in Tobago, the Caribbean and Stepney, East London in the late sixties, I have marvelled at the ability of young people not only to reach out and empathise with others in faraway places of the world, but through their ever-incisive imaginations to emulate each other's forms and modes of poetic expression within the universality of childhood.

In Tyendinaga, I used poems written by British inner-city children of Sheffield – mainly of Pakistani origins – as the stimulus to encourage the writing of poetry by the young Mohawk Canadians. In Britain I had commonly employed the life experiences of Chileans, South Africans, Palestinians, Angolans, Turkish migrant workers in Germany or Mexicans in California, Omanis, the Irish of

216

Belfast, Namibians and Native Americans to prompt the imaginative and empathetic instincts of my students.

Now, in taking the lives of young Sheffielders to a Mohawk reservation school in Canada, I was seeking to extend this cultural and geographical process of the imagination in ways none of us could have imagined during the early to mid-nineties, when Sheffield poems had been forged in a Pitsmoor classroom.

Many of these Sheffield poets were teenagers of Pakistani origins. Their parents' homelands had been in Mirpur and Kashmir, where their families had been subsistence farmers. 'I was born in a very remote village where donkeys were the main form of transportation and buying bricks to build a house was out of people's reach entirely,' declared one Pakistani pioneer migrant. 'We were peasants and toiled as labourers day and night worrying about not having enough to eat.' Although the original intention had been to come to South Yorkshire 'just for five years,' and return with enough money to improve their families' lives, many settled into a new life in Sheffield. 'I came to Sheffield for the work,' declared another father, 'but perhaps this city has become my home. I remember the English people I've worked with in Sheffield. I cannot think of the possibility of living outside Sheffield. This is my home.' Despite the struggles – to find regular work, and somewhere to live, to unite their families and resist racism, Pakistani newcomers found a living as steelworkers, taxi drivers and transport workers. Others saved earnings and bought premises for fast-food restaurants, halal butchers or small shops in the Pitsmoor and Fir Vale neighbourhoods. Their children grew up as bilingual Sheffielders, speaking Panjabi at home and Sheffieldese English at school.

In 1784, a group of 110 Mohawks who had sided with the British during the American War of Independence arrived at the Bay of Quinte, a large inlet into Lake Ontario, to establish the Tyendinaga Territory within Canada. They had escaped from the Mohawk Valley in what now is upstate New York, and chose for their home a former fishing village, believed to be the home of a past peacemaker, Deganawidha, surrounded by rolling countryside that was potentially rich agricultural land.

Succeeding generations built up a stable and prosperous farming community in Tyendinaga, with some men frequently following the Mohawk tradition of working outside the territory – particularly as iron workers on high-rise construction sites, where teams of Mohawks established a formidable reputation in erecting the steel frames for skyscrapers in many American and Canadian cities, especially in New York, Chicago and Toronto.

Now, in the first decade of the 21st century, Mohawk children completed their elementary education (until the eighth grade) at their reservation school before moving on to high schools in the towns outside the Tyendinaga Territory, usually in the adjacent town of Belleville.

In my classes I decided to read with them a series of poems written by my ex-students of Pitsmoor and Fir Vale about the places where they lived, their neighbourhoods and the people with whom they lived, their families, neighbours and communities. These poems had strong observational and critical dimensions, and I wondered how they would be received in a local school of what was a tightly-knit reservation community, administered by the locally elected band, or council. In my classes in Sheffield I had deliberately employed the writing of poetry at school as a means of sharpening both use of language and critical consciousness: using the condensed and meaning-laden dimension of poetical language as a vehicle for understanding the pressures and forces bearing down on the young poets' lives and those of their families, friends and communities. The principle was that such clear, concise and frequently figuratively-emphatic language must tell the truth of the local world as the poets saw it all around them, whether in Pitsmoor, Fir Vale and the other neighbourhoods of north-east Sheffield – or now in Tyendinaga. These worlds had two primary constituents. The first was the physical world of buildings, streets, houses, open places –

whether referred to with pride, condemnation or critical insight, seen with fear or love, vandalised or beautified. The other was the life within; the people who lived there, those who sought to humanise the material world – and their continuous impact upon each other.

From anthologies of poetry published at Earl Marshal during the early nineties: *Valley of Words* and *Heart of Sheffield*, I distributed and read out loud a number of these Fir Vale and Pitsmoor poems. Here was Sajida's poem, *Fir Vale*:

I was lying in my bed
And I was looking at a book
That I just read.
It was about a very nice place called Fir Vale –
Well, according to the book, anyway!
It was so different from the real Fir Vale,
It had clean and tidy roads,
No smashed windows covered with boards.
There wasn't any litter
And everyone was much, much fitter.
Children were playing
Their parents were praying –
Then I thought about the real Fir Vale
And litter on the streets,
Parks without any seats,
People being called racist names
And no children playing any games.
What kind of place is this?
It's a place you can never miss!

And I followed this with Fozya's poem,

Pitsmoor

I am Pitsmoor
where there is robbery
I am Pitsmoor
where there is burglary
burnt cars here
broken windows there.
I am Pitsmoor
where there is violence

I am Pitsmoor
where there are people
ruining our environment
Being racist there
Broken bottles there.
I am Pitsmoor
where people shout
'black people should get lost!
and so should women!'
I am Pitsmoor
that has a heart too.

Raksana and Nazia combined to write about their street, rendering it a human voice and sensitivity – and becoming it in a poetic act of unusual empathy:

The Street that No-one Cares About

I am the street of Idsworth Road,
I am the street which has got broken bottles on it,
I am the street that has a pub on it,
I am the street where muggers hang about,
I am the street where dogs bark,
I am the street of troubled people,
I am the street of Idsworth Road.
I am like a prisoner
People dump things on me
They don't know I have a life.
I can feel the children play on me
I can feel the heat of the sun
I can feel the pain
When glass bottles are smashed on me.
I am the street of Idsworth Road.

Poems such as these made a strong impression on the Tyendinaga children. Some of them commented that they thought that poetry was not like this, but should be a 'cleaner' way of writing. Its subject matter should be about prettier or more fantastical things. They had not been introduced to its dimension of social realism or verisimilitude. Others had no idea that England could be so. Some Mohawks still saw England as the Crown and protector, festooned within the colonial propaganda that it was always the source of things just and fair. How could there be such places as Pitsmoor in England, with its urban desperation, violence and vandalism – and where so many young people were not white and had such 'un-English' names? The territory had lived through two resolutely Christian and Anglican centuries and sentimental contacts with the British royal family – and union jacks were still to be found flying from houses and gardens. So suddenly, here was a very different and surprising perspective arising from these young Pakistani-Sheffield poets, and one not present in the Mohawk children's conventional impressions of this faraway and royal land. Thus in a similar way that the Pitsmoor poems had the effect of stripping away illusions about the Sheffield children's part of their city – the streets and estates where they lived, they also demonstrated to the Tyendinaga children how poetry could be a means of clearing the mind and perceptions of deception and falsity, cutting below the surfaces and setting down a true picture and meanings both about the place where you live and the people who live there with you.

So how did the Tyendinaga children respond? They began in quietness and concentration to write about their own world, so different yet so similar to that of the children a continent and ocean away who had provoked them. Dani, for example, wrote a portrait of the 'Rez' that was affirmative, even endearing about its people, yet with a subliminal critical view:

The Rez

The Rez is a wonderful place
Birds sing so beautifully in the morning,
All day long
People work hard for their money
And children read and write very well.
But there is a down side
There are drugs and alcohol,

221

There are cigarettes and bullies
And being bullied by a native kid
Is worse than anything.
You didn't want to be here three months ago
Before we got help.
There is a man called Jagar, or Dave
As we all know him,
He taught us that way
Was the wrong way to go.
Now we're getting better at it
The streets are more peaceful and quiet
The skies are blue
The clouds are clean
And we've even got flowers growing.
The Rez is a wonderful place,
Birds sing so beautifully in the morning
All day long,
People work hard for their money
And children read and write very well.
I'd love it to stay this way,
But it won't, I know it won't.

Several students wrote about their 'subdivision,' a new
neighbourhood where, despite appearances, problems lurk
behind a deceptive front. This is Cassandra's poem:

Living in the Subdivision

Living in the subdivision, you look around,
at first everything seems quiet, no-one makes a sound,
everything seems clean until you look down
and see scattered trash all over the ground.
At night while most people are sleeping
Trouble emerges as the druggies start creeping,
keeping a low profile, leaving when the lost child
starts weeping.
Across the street there's a robbery
depending on reputation, everyone starts asking me
they play mind games, this isn't how they're supposed to be.
Rumours, gossip, manipulating and more
Sometimes I think these people don't know what
they are living for,
arguing and fighting, around here backstabbing
is so hardcore.

Some people say here is beautiful, others say it sucks,
don't be fooled by the views, or people who
try acting tough,
they get scared when someone comes along
who's just as rough -
then there's the innocent who dare not strut their
stuff,
certain instigators get people saying they've
'had enough.'
Living in the subdivision, you've got to be half-happy,
half sad -
this part of the reservation is part good and half bad,
sometimes I wanna scream, it gets me so mad.

Other poets sought to emulate the Pitsmoor children's efforts to empathise with the place where they lived – to become it through their imaginations. Thus, *I am Pitsmoor* became *I am Tyendinaga* for Stephanie:

I am Tyendinaga
where it's noisy,
where birds come and go.
I am Tyendinaga
where it's full of trash.
No one takes care of me
I feel sad, full of pity.
I am Tyendinaga
Where flowers bloom
where sunrises and sunsets begin
where the sky is pure blue
I am Tyendinaga
where the sun shines bright

and for Devon too, who wrote:

I am Tyendinaga
I am the one where you find many things
I am the one where you find drugs
I am the one where you find vandalism
I am the one where you find poorness.
But I'm also the one where you'll find a heart
I am the one where you'll find love
I am the one where you'll find a home
I'm the one.

Eli used this 'Pitsmoor' form to set down issues of conflict and racism over hunting and fishing rights with those outside the reservation:

I am Tyendinaga
A river flows on my back
People hunt and fish
Like we should.
I feel the animals.
Long green grass,
where only a couple of people have been.
There's lots of racism
when the people fish off my back.
There's lots of protesting
to try to get our rights back.
Sometimes it's handled well
Other times cops and swat teams are there.
When people protest off my back
I can protect them the best I can
When they're on my back.

Ryan extended the idea of Tyendinaga's world 'on my back' to reflections of the indigenous Mohawk creation story of the world beginning from a woman's making on the shell of a turtle. This was expressed as a proud mural from the ceiling to floor along the school's main corridor outside his classroom. He continues by telling of the conquest and desecration of this world by European powers, and his poem takes on a critical/historical perspective as the turtle becomes the narrator and griot of his people's, and much of the world's oppressions and struggles:

I am Turtle Island
I am Turtle Island, I'm long and wide
I used to be free of garbage, drugs, rubble
and turmoil,
We did not know of war before Europe
sailed across the sea.
French, British and Americans fought over
land that was free.
For First Nations that land could not be owned

They fought over it like it was a small piece
of gold,
Up to this very day they fight over it.
They put First Nations on small reservations
And gave us a bad name.
I'm now very littered, drugs are all over my back.
They've made names for different parts
of my back
Like Canada and the United States
And the different towns and cities.
There's wars, drugs, disease, death and prisons,
Nothing is good any more.
Sometimes I wish that Europe never
crossed the water,
Maybe then my back could be way
more clean.

Ryan's powerful poem held within it centuries of invasion, colonisation, apartheid and struggle: the theft of the lands of the indigenous American peoples, the imposition of the reservation system; the creation of frontiers and external political entities across their territories; the despoliation of their lands and the attempts to destroy their reputation and culture; the introduction by European settlement of previously unknown deadly diseases, drugs and environmental catastrophe. The aboriginal writer Keith Matthews declared: 'Non-native Canadians don't understand the sordid, hidden history of Canada.' But Ryan does. All this is condensed into a poem by a fourteen-year-old Mohawk boy, using the legends and stories of his own ancestors, inspired to write poetry by a group of Pakistani Sheffielders a continent and an ocean away, now living in the land of their original colonisers. Such is the power of poetry as a messenger and lever.

If *I am Turtle Island* invoked such stories from history, a poem by another Pitsmoor schoolgirl about her grandmother became the inspiration of a series of Mohawk children's very personal poems about their own elders and parents. In 1992, in an Earl Marshal classroom, Zaibun had written this poem about her grandmother:

My Grandmother

When I think about my grandmother
I get tears in my eyes.
I remember when she used to tell me off,
Not to point.
She used to say, 'Don't you do that,
It's very rude.'
I used to ignore her
and cry, cry and cry.
She used to get mad
and so did I,
She used to hug me
and cry.
Now I think, oh!
Why did I make her cry?
And I feel very sorry for her
And I don't ignore her now.
She was tall, thin
and had long, long hair
with a beautiful face
and small feet –
Oh! I do think about her!

It moved the Tyendinaga children in 2005 with its memories of love and loss more than any other which we read and studied, and provoked some strong responses. Nine-year-old Kayla wrote immediately:

Me and My Grandmother

Me and my grandmother
used to go to pow-wow together.
But now we don't
because she passed away
not too long ago.
I used to native dance for her
in my leather dress
with my jewellery.
I danced
many different dances,
she loved it
when I danced

for her.
I miss those times.

While Keenan remembered dramatic and happy fishing times with his grandfather:

My Grandfather

My grandfather and I went fishing.
One day
we caught some big ones
some small ones.
Some were pickerel, and some were pike.
Then suddenly I got a really big bite
My grandfather said, 'reel fast!!!'
When I got it in
It was a huge sheep head!!!
So I started to yell
'can we eat it?
can we eat it?'
Then my grandfather said
'No, it has too many bones' –
so we started to fish again.

Dakota remembered exhilarating fishing forays with his mother, this time by the traditional method of spearing in the fast-flowing waters that run into the Bay of Quinte:

Spearing with My Mum

Spearing is fun
Spearing is neat,
I like it because you get lots of meat.
I think spearing is a treat,
You don't even know when the fish are coming
But when they do, spear them too!
I go spearing with my mum
I think spearing is lots of fun!

Some of the poems of family expressed a certain sadness along with pride in absent fathers, working for long periods away from the reservation. One boy wrote

about his ironworker father, another about his dream
of ironworking:

My Dad the Ironworker

My dad works all over the place
He works all different parts of Canada and America
My dad is an ironworker.
He works on a lot of cool buildings
like the Detroit Tigers' stadium
I never really get to see him
only on weekends
When he is home we have lots of
Good and bad times –
That's my Dad, the Native Ironworker

High and Mighty

I wish to be an ironworker,
build a building so high and tall.
I would be king of the world,
So high and mighty, yet peaceful.
And quiet, I'm not afraid of heights,
and I live for dangerous things.
From atop the high towers
people look like ants, itty-bitty and small.
What a great job to be high and mighty!

And Stephanie wrote about her trucker father, so often
away:

My Dad

Nine years ago my dad was a truck driver
Oh how I missed him on his long trips to the States.
Mostly, we never had any time to spend together,
I missed him a lot.
He was gone for a week or two
We couldn't even play ball hockey or catch or soccer.
I felt lonely at times
I always looked at the windows
Waiting for him to come home.
Now he has a new job
Now I don't have to wait or worry anymore.

228

And John's poem of his father is more about the man who gave him his haircut – proudly and exquisitely in the Mohawk style:

> When my Dad gives me a haircut
> he asks me to sit in a chair
> and he puts a towel on me.
> He uses a razor to cut my hair,
> he makes it so it looks like a Mohawk.
> He cuts both sides
> and in the middle there is hair.
> When it gets too long
> he cuts it to a Mohawk again.
> Sometimes it hurts
> Sometimes it didn't hurt
> but it makes my eyeballs fall out.

A subliminal text to these poems were the national statistics concerning young aboriginal people in Canada: the strongly disproportionate levels of alcoholism – including foetal alcohol syndrome, of school drop-outs, of drug addiction, of youth suicides. Two poems by Kayla and Lacy offered a sense of optimism and tenacity from the heat of these prevailing oppressions, with Lacy still employing the 'first person' methods he had read in the Pitsmoor poems. First, Kayla:

Never Give Up

> Life has lots of ups and downs
> Lots of smiles and frowns
> Lots of straight and rough edges
> but you should never give up.
> Suicide is not the only way out,
> problems come both good and bad,
> but don't give up, don't be sad.
> Just make the best of what you have
> and love life good or bad.

Then Lacy:

> I am the world
> the world that could be a better place.

I am the world
the world with kids at the age of seven swearing,
And taking control of their parents.
I am the world
The world with fourteen year-old young
women getting pregnant.
I am the world
the world that has violence
the world that has to change
hoping soon the war is over
and people stop doing bad habits
and getting an education.
I am the world that hopefully changes soon.

An afterword: in February 2020 Tyendinaga protesters were mounting a solidarity blockade, stopping trains on the Canadian National Rail line at Belleville, Ontario, the closest town to Tyendinaga, where I had caught the train back to Toronto, They were responding to the call for support by hereditary chiefs of the Wet'suet'on first nation of British Columbia – thousands of miles west, who were opposing a 670 kilometre natural gas pipeline crossing their territory without consent. They had called for solidarity protests by indigenous peoples across the huge nation. Protests on railway lines, at ferry terminals, on roads and at government offices by native Canadians ensued. As I read the press reports of the Tyendinaga blockade and police arrests, I realised that the protesters were those very young poets who had written so powerfully, now in their late twenties. A mother of one of them proudly declared: 'All the natives across Canada are standing together. I like that! They're standing together in solidarity.'

In 2006, a collection of my poems, *Lightning of Your Eyes* was published by Smokestack Press and launched in the Marx Memorial Library at Clerkenwell Green, London. What pleased me most was when a large minibus pulled up outside the museum and a dozen or so of my Yemeni friends and students walked in – from straight down the M1, two-hundred miles away, from Attercliffe now in the teeming heart of London. As I read and talked about my poems, I looked down and saw them all there, friends from Stepney and the Basement Writers to Pitsmoor and Attercliffe, and marvelled how the poetical spirit had unified my life. I read this poem, dedicated to Abdul's dad who had recently passed and for all the Yemenis, and I hoped they knew how much they had given to me – and I only wished that I knew Arabic so I could put it all into their words too:

Poem for Shaif

Old man on a stony Yorkshire hill,
Warm and friendly Arab of steel
Size belying the power of the mind
Now at the end of your journey
You look over your valley of a working life
Over demolished foundries, uprooted rolling mills
Furnaces doused by history, forever melted steel
After the miles through crag and sea and land
Through a canal reclaimed by brothers,
Arab with laughing, radiant eyes
Man of Yemen, elder of Sheffield
Two places of living, but one life
Two sets of hills but one mountain climbed
A colonial power repulsed, a partition repelled
A village from the rocks to a city of sleeting streets
From the stepped farm terraces to foreign factory gantries
A village to leave, a far community to build
A people to unite, a world to win.
You went some way, old man of Shaibi,
And those who leave and love you
Will carry on your journey.

When Bill Moore died in July 2008 at 94 years of age, I knew I had lost a true friend. The last time I saw him was just before I went back to Toronto. The Yemenis had given me a Palestinian scarf, and I wanted to give it to Bill. I went to his flat overlooking the Sheffield to London railway line as I had done dozens of times before, and he made me his customary cup of very strong coffee in a huge cup. As he sat down, I put the scarf around his neck. Ever the internationalist, he was both surprised and delighted. As I left, he was wearing it proudly and I shall always remember him in that way, the Chartist spirit of Samuel Holberry burning in his eyes.

Chapter 8
A World of Hope to Walk in

My last paid job, which I began when I returned from Canada in 2007, was at Manchester University as Director of the Ahmed Iqbal Ullah Race Relations Resource Centre. Ahmed had been killed by a fellow pupil in the playground of Burnage High School, Manchester on 17th September 1986, and through the tireless work of Lou Kushnick, a sociology professor at the university, this Centre had been set up in his name, to work and campaign against racism within the University and the City's schools.

For me, taking the train across the Pennines on the Hope Valley Line early in the morning and arriving in Manchester at eight o'clock, wasn't a bad way to start off the day, looking out the window at the Peak District after we passed through the Totley Tunnel, seeing Grindleford and Hathersage where I was still playing cricket in the summer months, through the Hope Valley and Edale, and eventually through Stockport to Manchester. It was a beautiful awakening, all through the year. I became close friends with the Centre's librarian, Ruth, and regular visitors like Barrington Young – eighty years young, who had arrived from Jamaica in the fifties, worked for British Rail for nearly half a century, and became the first black inspector on its northern train routes. Still a veteran campaigner we had our weekly discussions about the Caribbean and Britain with many a cup of tea and plate of biscuits between us.

In July 2008 Nelson Mandela would be ninety, so we decided to mark his life and achievement by a book of poems by Manchester school children. *Mandela, Manchester* we called it, and as I wrote in its preface, it was 'the city's tribute to a great human being of the Twentieth Century, whose example shines for all those who will build their lives within the century that follows.' These weren't poems about Mandela, they were about Manchester, but as Rachel put it in her poem *Mandela in Manchester,* they were certainly about Mandela's inspiration:

His spirit is here
Not the man himself.
It's in and around Manchester
And also in yourself.

I went all around the city to create poetry workshops in many of its schools, like the giant comprehensive Parrs Wood to the tiny special school where a thirteen year old boy called Menelik with his rolling locks wrote this poem with a huge nod to Mandela's Africa:

Menelik

My name is Menelik
I am the King
I am the people
I am the Emperor of Ethiopia
I am the human
I am powerful
When the Italian army invaded
     our country
I led my people
We stopped the Italians
     and sent them back
My grandmother is a Rastafarian
She thought of my name
My grandmother loves the African
     people.

And there, anonymous, left on a desk at Abraham Moss School, was this poem:

The Dad I Can Never See :

The dad I can never see,
He left me when I was three.
I used to wish at night

That my dad would come
out with a fright.

The dad I can never see,
He left me when I was three.
He used to always tuck me in
at night
And always say 'sleep tight.'

The dad I can never see,
He left me when I was three.
I miss my dad
I wish he could come out of jail
I want to see my dad.

Sibongile Mkhabele of the Nelson Mandela Children's
Fund, where any money from the anthology went, wrote in
the introduction: 'Through this anthology, the city of
Manchester is storming into the corridors of literacy excellence through its children', and at the launching, in the
huge muralled hall of Manchester Town Hall, that would
have been difficult to deny as the young poets, one after the
other, read out their poems.

For me, I had memories of four decades before and
Stepney Words. There were similar contradictions, similar
ambivalences. There was Sam Hughes and his alienated
vision of a city:

I am Manchester

I am Manchester
I am the howling at night,
It is I who has the respect
        of nothingness,
Like the child that seems to take
The rocky path,
The child who uses violence
And resorts to guns.
I am the demon within this world,
I am the source of hurt and pain.
I am Manchester
The left-out Manchester

But there was nothing left out in Anthony Hall's rampaging *Cheetham Hill;* full of everyone, everyone's chorus:

Cheetham Hill it is just one of those places,
Full of different religions and different races.
We all come together to join as one,
Cheetham Hill, Cheetham Hill that's where
     I am from.

I'm not trying to say it's easy because I
     know life's hard,
There is abuse and racism, emotions are
     scarred.
We all come together to join as one,
Cheetham Hill, Cheetham Hill that's where
     I am from.

Yobs, crimes, everybody wants justice,
     not to be hurt.
And the end of the day we're human, not
     dirt.
We all come together to join as one.
Cheetham Hill, Cheetham Hill that's where
     I am from.

We all live together and breathe each
     other's air,
All we want is to be treated fair.
Cheetham Hill, Cheetham Hill, that's
     where I am from.
We all come together to join as one.

The spirit of Ahmed Iqbal Ullah, of Nelson Mandela and of Manchester young people all over the city, 'all come together and joined as one' that evening in their poems, and the Victorian neo-gothic grandeur of the Town Hall rocked with joy.

I finally retired in 2012, but set myself a number of urgent writing and publishing tasks to complete. The first was to collect together and find a publisher for the poems of my old friend Peter Blackman, who had died in 1993, still without any volume of his poems ever being published.

Andy Croft and Smokestack Books obliged with a beautiful publication. I called the collection *Footprints*. In his greatest poem, *My Song is for All Men* of 1952 he declared that the black man's and woman's 'footprints are nowhere in history'. Well, I thought, Peter's are definitely there now, never to be erased. My second task was to complete my collection of jazz essays from the *Morning Star*. I called it *Red Groove* and my old friend Robert Wyatt wrote an introduction. It was my second book on jazz. *Forward Groove,* which sought to situate the

music in the real political world of the struggle against racism and war in the USA, Britain and South Africa was published in 2008 and it was launched in Ray's Jazz in the heart of Foyles' bookshop in Charing Cross Road and with an interview in the lobby of Queen Elizabeth Hall at the London Jazz Festival.

The menace of school exclusions was still rife in Sheffield schools, even in 2016, some two decades after the Earl Marshal furore. This time it was being targeted at new residents of Fir Vale, Page Hall and Darnall, the Slovak Roma families who had begun to settle in Sheffield from 2004 onwards when Slovakia became part of the European Union. By 2015 there were 567 Roma / Slovak students in Sheffield schools and in the same year 148 of these had been excluded – a grotesque reality, founded upon a vicious institutional racism and anti-Roma revival, greater even than the children of black communities had faced in the Seventies and Eighties. It hadn't been helped by David

Blunkett's tabloid interventions in the *Daily Star,* under the November 13, 2013 headline *Roma migrant invasion will start U.K. Riots.*

I had done some teaching in the Yemeni Attercliffe inclusion centre, which was caring for and educating many of the excluded Roma children, and I wrote a long article on the situation for *Race & Class* called *Xeno-racism and the Scourge of Roma School Exclusion,* developing Sivanandan's insights about this new brand of non-colour-coded racism aimed at 'the displaced, the dispossessed, and the uprooted, a xenophobia that bears all the marks of the old racism.' I interviewed several excluded children who described the incidents that provoked their exclusion: 'Even though there were cameras in that school and everyday they were provoking me,' said one girl, 'calling me a smelly Slovak and telling me they didn't want me in their country, the teachers didn't stop them.' And proud and defiant, one of the boys said that others in his class shouted at him: 'Fucking go back to your own country. So I fought them. I'm not going to let that pass, am I?' The Sheffield Education Department's response to the article was to deny its facts and arguments and threaten to withdraw precious funding from the Yemeni inclusion initiative. I wondered how much had changed.

In 2016 I was contacted by the East London arts organisation, Rich Mix, which had an idea about collecting together a new collection of poems by children in Tower Hamlets schools. They had discovered the story of *Stepney Words* and wanted to revisit its original conception with a new, now-times anthology. In 1971 Ron McCormick and I had already done *Stepney Words* and *Stepney Words No.2,* so this new collection was going to be called *Stepney Words III.* Ron had lived in Newport, South Wales for many years, but was still up for doing the photographs and design, so off we went. Rich Mix found four young 'spoken word' poets to create workshops in four secondary schools: Morpeth, Bethnal Green Academy, George Green's and my old school in the Seventies, Langdon

Park, and I did a classroom session in all four of them, loving every moment. Ron and I came back to East London for a week or so, and did what we had done nearly fifty years earlier, walking the streets, talking in cafes while Ron snapped with his third eye anything that deserved a picture. He hadn't changed, engaging his potential subjects with his quips and conversation while he made their humanity permanent and unique through the power and artistry of his lens. We even went to the top floor of Latham House, tower block next to Sir John Cass School and Ron pointed his camera at the same place where he had photographed the bleak, sepia cityscape with its shining river gleaming, that had formed the front cover of the original *Stepney Words* in 1971. Now it was the banks and high rises of Canary Wharf and the millionaires' havens, sprouting from what had been derelict docks and rusty cranes that formed the image of 1971 even though the same terrace houses of Bromley Street still stood in the foreground. We stared from that top eminence and marvelled at the changes. And the photograph Ron took, became the front cover of *Stepney Words III*, some forty-six years later.

As for the poems they were both very different and very similar to those in the original *Stepney Words*. When I read the brief and lucid *Random* by Hana Abdi, I thought; 'That could have been written in 1971, so universal and word-struck is it, so riven is it with contradiction.'

loved, but alone
scared, but safe
hurt, but happy
broken , but together
a happy ever after
has never been
forever

When I did my session in Langdon Park, I explained how I had been an English teacher there four and a half decades before, and how I had lived near the school on the Aberfeldy

Estate, in Blackwall, and how brave the Bangladeshi families were who lived there, often within the hateful scourge of racism. Two girls raised their hands: 'We live there, sir!' they said. One of them, Ishrat, wrote this: It's in *Stepney Words III,* opposite Ron's beautiful photograph of a teenage Asian girl:

I am not different

I come from Britain but I am Asian
My roots are from Bangladesh
I live in Aberfeldy
I celebrate Eid and Ramadan
I study in a mixed school
with people like me and people not like me
I am not different

The community is one
Like a big family but there are some
        people who are outsiders
We face many challenges together
and many new experiences
We have events for youngsters and the
        elderly
I am not different

I feel safe
with people who are behind me
This is my hood!
Lots of people have my back, so watch out
' coz this is where I belong.
I am not different

East London girl
East London is my world
and where I come from
So remember, I am not different.

It was that proud belongingness, that she was unambiguously an 'East London girl' that was new. And then I remembered that the Bangladeshi arrivant children that I used to teach in these same classrooms could be their fathers – or maybe their grandmothers. And when her friend Fateha declared the same confidence and belonging

240

in her poem, as she read it to her class I could only feel proud and joyous inside:

Reality

> I come from...
> a plughole, which pulls you into -
> the world of stereotypes
> No choice just opinions
> Are boys really superior?
> Is my race a barrier?
> Maybe, maybe not
> but it's my life.

> I come from...
> a war between desperate
> civilians fighting for their
> place on the estate
> but it's my home.

> I come from...
> a place where help lies free
> where hospitals and schools -
> are gifts from the government
> where freedom means peace
> where a community is a family
> that's my life!

> I come from a place...
> where education goes without money
> where quality outweighs quantity
> where the surprises are neverending
> I am proud to say...
> I come from East London.

I walked out of the school like I had done a thousand times all those years before, thinking how lucky I was. I looked for the pub we used to go to and it wasn't there any more. Even that didn't seem to matter when I thought of the pride and consciousness of Ishrat and Fateha: Aberfeldy girls, Aberfeldy promise.

A month or so later, the first part of my autobiography, *Isaac and I*, was published, called so because of the

241

lifelong relationship I have had with the life and poetry of Isaac Rosenberg, the Stepney poet killed in 1918 during the final weeks of the First World War. At the launch in Tower Hamlets History Library at Mile End, many of my Stepney ex-students were there, now in their sixties, those who had gone on strike in May 1971 when I was sacked from Sir John Cass and Redcoat School for publishing their poems in *Stepney Words*. Much of the autobiography described these events and my fight for reinstatement, which finally came to pass in 1973, and the BBC nightly programme, *The One Show* filmed a feature on the strike, using the 1971 footage, and interviewing three of my old students and myself in the school – the first time I had been back inside its walls since 1973. The programme's director asked my former students and some present day students at the school to write a collective poem which she would film us reading in the church opposite the school, the same church whose vicar had been chair of the school's governors who had sacked me in 1971. It hadn't been hallowed ground to me! We each wrote a couplet, which were joined together, and this was the end result, which went out on the BBC television show a few days later. It was called simply, *Stepney*, written by four sixteen-year-olds, three sixty-year-olds and one seventy-three-year-old:

Back in Stepney, after forty-six years
Fond memories of great times, grazed
    knees and a few tears.
Wapping-on-Thames two minutes from here
Today back in Stepney, my London home
    I hold dear.
Came back home, all alone,
Parents gone, my sister's moved on.
To walk through our streets, adjusting
    to everything in sight,
The comfort of being home carries
    me through the night.

Mixed into the community of delightful
  surprises
The eyes that all tell different stories
  see the same sunrises.
We were all born from this seed
And all grow up, sticking to our creed.
A rich jewel, sparkling in excellence,
We thrive in one body, precious and eminent.
Intense diversity and extreme solidarity,
Bring us tranquillity and a sense of serenity.
Children of Stepney, your lives flow with the
  Thames,
The world is in your words, the future in
  your flames.

It was a telling event. In 1971 the school had a few Black
and mixed race children, but the overwhelming majority
was white. Now, walking around the school, I hardly saw a
white student: almost all were Black and Asian, mostly
Somali and Bangladeshi. Such is East London, ever internationalist, always cosmopolitan. It seemed that the
poetical spirit, human and generous, was one of the few
constants, embedded still within the hearts of the now-
times Stepney poets who had read their words so movingly,
nearly half a century after another generation of young
poets had been on strike for theirs.

One last book, one last reading, I thought, and before I
felt compelled to write this one I had always wanted to
write a short study of the work of my first poetical hero,
Isaac Rosenberg. So my book *Whitechapel Boy* was part
critical, part praise-song, part a commemoration of the
hundredth anniversary of his murder, like millions of
others, by King, whiskey generals like Haig and arms profiteers who sent him and his generation, in my family too, to
agony and death in the trenches. The book was an
amalgam of my words on Isaac and his slaughtered genius
of language and poetry, and Ron's wonderful photographs
of the dying Jewish world of Spitalfields and Whitechapel

where he had forged his art in the early seventies, and we had published *Stepney Words* together. At the local history library in Bancroft Road, just off Mile End Road where Isaac and his friends, who were known as the Whitechapel Boys, would take their long nightly walks after Whitechapel Library closed, we launched the book. Joseph Leftwich, poet, Yiddish scholar and diarist; David Bomberg and Mark Gertler, painters; John Rodker, Stephen Winsten, poets: these were the young men, Jews and socialists, who were the Whitechapel Boys and Isaac's closest friends. I read his greatest poem, *Dead Man's Dump* and tried to find words to describe his genius. His nephew Bernard Wynick was there, son of his sister Annie who would lovingly type up the poems that he sent home from the trenches. Just before I began my talk I received an email from Jeremy Corbyn, now leader of the Labour party and fellow devotee of Isaac, wishing me every strength for the launching and telling me of his deep love of his poetry. 'Very impressed with your interview with Ben Cowles in the *Morning Star* today. I cannot wait to read *Whitechapel Boy*,' he wrote. 'I am a great admirer of Isaac Rosenberg and read one of his poems at Remembrance Sunday last year. A young poverty-stricken Jewish man who suffered anti-semitic abuse and wrote with such brilliance and humanity and in the horrors of the trenches was writing to free Africans from oppression and subjugation. Like so many brilliant people who lost their lives in World War One, we can only imagine what they could have achieved.'

I felt that I had reached out to Isaac and his humanity, and found him again. So I finish this second part of my life story with the poet with whom I began the first: with Isaac whose words and spirit have given me so much for over half a century.

AFTERWORD

One other essential retirement project which I set for myself was to somehow republish the poems of the militant suffragette and socialist revolutionary, Sylvia Pankhurst, which had originally been published in 1921 by the paper which Sylvia edited, the *Workers Dreadnought*. In 1974 we had used her poems to stimulate our children in our Poplar classrooms, after we had discovered a rare copy of her collection *Writ on Cold Slate* in the Tower Hamlets Local History Library in Mile End. Helped by the brilliant local librarian, Bernard Nurse, who photocopied the poems for us, we found that they had been written during Sylvia's time in Holloway Prison, where she had been incarcerated for sedition for her non-stop anti-war activism in East London, and her support for local dockers who were refusing to to load weapons to be used against the Soviet Union on ships intended for Russia. Denied pens and other writing materials in Holloway, she wrote her poems on slate so her gaolers could summarily wash them away into oblivion. Yet they somehow survived and had been published, but never republished during the century that followed. When I showed them in 2019 to Andy Croft, poetry editor of the *Morning Star*, he published them again through his imprint, Smokestack Press. We set the poems side by side with the powerful photographs of her suffragette comrade, Norah Smyth. They had so much to tell and teach us after a century in the darkness, and as I held the 2021 edition of *Writ on Cold Slate* in my hands it was as if Sylvia was standing next to me, telling me again of the ceaseless struggle and achievement of working women.

But more was to come. In November 2021, during a window of the pandemic, East London's local university, Queen Mary University of London, along the Mile End Road where Isaac had walked, talked and read his poems under the gaslight to the other Whitechapel Boys more

245

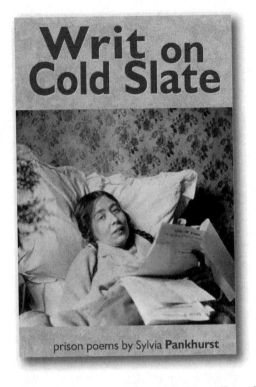

Writ on Cold Slate

prison poems by Sylvia **Pankhurst**

than a century before on their nightly walks after the Whitechapel Library closed its doors – organised a symposium called 'Stepney Words 50 Years On', as part of their Being Human Festival, in partnership with the Raphael Samuel History Centre. Professor Nadia Valman of the Urban Literature Project and BBC radio documentary maker Alan Dein put the event together at the People's Palace, now a part of the University, where the *Stepney Words* poets had read their poems in April 1971, at the Festival of Racial Harmony, organised by the pioneering anti-racist campaigner born in St. Vincent, Joe Hunte, then chair of the Council of Citizens of Tower Hamlets, whose brave writings had exposed the racism within the Metropolitan Police.

Nadia and Alan were determined that the ex-Sir John Cass and Redcoat School (renamed Stepney All Saints School) should be centrally involved, and the new leadership of the school, headteacher Paul Woods and chair of governors Angela Saunders, were enthusiastic in their response. In October 2021 I was invited to lead several poetry workshops with the students of the school, along with four of the original *Stepney Words* poets now in their mid-sixties: Sharon Harrison, Karen Crowther, Kim McGee and Jimmy Went. The workshops produced some moving poems by the now-times thirteen-year-old poets, and for me, teaching poems written fifty years before in the same classrooms – including Lesley Samuels' beautiful *Autumn Morning in Stepney Churchyard*, was an experience I had only ever dreamed of. After the workshops, as I walked out of the school and through the churchyard, I looked up at the trees and down at the 'ever lay leaves', remembering Lesley's lyrical cadence, 'falling, falling, falling' with the just-written poem of Harriet Johnstone's still in my head and her line about the 'fiery leaves' of autumn:

Stepney Autumn Morning

My fiery leaves lay fallen
The cheeky squirrels play,

Always looking down.
In the meanwhile the burning sun
Glimmers through my matchstick branches.

The birds sing with glee,
We seem to be in the country.

People wake
The sun is dawning
On this Stepney autumn morning

As I crossed Ben Jonson Road, next to the churchyard, I remembered the great poet and dramatist's lines which have stayed with me ever since university days: 'Give me a look/Give me a face/That makes simplicity a grace'. They took me back to the essential simplicity and lucidity of these young cosmopolitan poets' words, still ever-creating, ever-continuing. I walked up Whitehorse Lane to Stepney Green station as I had done hundreds of times fifty years before, passing Trafalgar Gardens, the setting of Khadija's brave poem, full of consciousness, pride and indignation following the murder of Sarah Everard in South London by a serving police officer a few weeks before, expressing the outrage of millions.

Trafalgar Park

In Trafalgar Gardens, in the broad daylight,
In the place I reside in, in the place I call home.
Security savagely snatched away from me.
'God damn, I'd love to take her home tonight!'
My body is covered up
But now it feels bare.
Now it's unsafe.
An innocent thirteen year old girl
Now seeming like a promiscuous prostitute?
Maybe I should cover up?
Maybe I asked for it?
The same places that gleam with my smile
Are the same place I've widened my eyes with horror.
And maybe I've been 'the girl asking for it' in your story,
But I'll always be the victim in mine,
My innocence stripped away from me
My happiness in the streets substituted with fear,
The fear the past me never knew about.
If ignorance is bliss, may I never know peace.

These same children read their poems alongside the 1971 poets at the symposium, where many old friends also contributed: Alan Gilbey and Tony Harcup revived the years of the Basement Writers, Ken Worpole spoke of the developments of working class writers' groups and an animated painting of the 1971 *Stepney Words* strike by the irrepressible Dan Jones was unveiled, soon to have pride of place in the entrance lobby of the re-named school. Lesley Samuels sent a visual message projected on the People's Palace's huge screen from her home in Perth, Western Australia, and in another filmed interview Cockney Rebel vocalist Steve Harley recalled how as a young *East London Advertiser* reporter, he had been dispatched by his editor to cover the strike in the pouring rain, after several young strikers had burst into the newspaper's offices along the Mile End Road, inviting the journalists to cover the resistance outside the school. For me it was uncanny: memory had become history, and I was old enough and lucky enough to experience the transition and see essential progress before my eyes, even in the crux of dark Covid times.

The symposium ended with the first screening of a film called *Stepney Words 50 Years On* made by the French filmmaker Berty Cadhilac and ended with a communal recitation of one of the original *Stepney Words* poem by Paul Ritchens, *Let it Flow Joe*. The People's Palace filled up with his words, as decades before it had resounded with the

immense power of Paul Robeson's voice. I could only reflect on their perennial meaning.

Let It Flow Joe

Let it flow Joe.
Let your feelings speak for you
Let the people know what you know

Tell the people what it's all about
Shout it out.

When you talk people come alive
People start to realise.

Words flow out of your mouth
When you talk about this earth
Tell the people everything Joe
About what you know.

Talk to them Joe
Let them know
Let the words flow out.